ANTE-BELLUM MANSIONS
OF ALABAMA

Ante-Bellum Mansions
of Alabama

by

RALPH HAMMOND

Photographs by the Author

Plans by Edwin B. Lancaster, A.I.A.

BONANZA BOOKS · NEW YORK

*This edition is published by Bonanza Books, a division
of Crown Publishers, Inc., by arrangement with the
Architectural Book Publishers, Inc.*
(R)

This book is dedicated to

MY MOTHER,

*Alice Holleman Hammond, whose life was as
beautiful as the homes pictured herein*

PRINTED IN THE UNITED STATES OF AMERICA

PREFACE

Selection of the houses to be included in this book was no easy task. In Alabama today, there are over two thousand ante-bellum houses which are of, or border on, the mansion type. Over three hundred were visited and personally studied. At least two hundred turned out to be typical and excellent.

Obviously, no such number could be adequately pictured and described in a book of convenient size and reasonable cost. So each notable old house was measured against the impartial yardstick of architectural excellence and sound construction. So measured, it became evident that fifty ante-bellum mansions and one more recent house, built in the old grand manner, simply could not be omitted.

This book grew out of my own conviction that, in these old houses, Alabama had fallen heir to a heritage of distinguished design and honest construction which should never be lost. In pictures and measured drawings their design at least, could be preserved indefinitely. Then it was not yet too late to dig out stories about the builders. That too seemed important, for these men were at the same time laying the foundations for the future great state. They knew very well what they were trying to create and to pass on. Perhaps a wider familiarity with their homes, these tangible surviving links with the past, may help us preserve it.

But if this book began as an attempt at preservation, it soon developed into a labor of love and ultimately into a constant inspiration, for as Keats said, "A thing of beauty is a joy forever."

RALPH HAMMOND

ACKNOWLEDGMENTS

THIS BOOK could never have been written, nor the photographs taken, had it not been for the hospitality of those who own the mansions. As a group they offered the utmost cooperation; as individuals they were cordial, helpful, eager to please, and most obliging: some have become constant and lasting friends, for which I am indeed grateful.

It is with humility and much gratitude that I extend my sincere thanks to them all. They are a part of this book. They deserve recognition. They are:

Mr. and Mrs. R. B. Kent; Mr. and Mrs. J. Innes Thornton; Misses Kate and Bessie Welch; Dr. and Mrs. J. D. McLeod; Misses Margaret and Ann and Mr. Joseph Hobson; Mr. and Mrs. Max Luther; Mr. and Mrs. H. H. Hammond; Mrs. Maria Ellis; Mrs. Jessie Winston Turnipseed; Mrs. Milton K. Cummins; Preferred Life Assurance Society; Dr. and Mrs. Berthold S. Kennedy; Mr. and Mrs. James F. Watts; Florence State Teachers College.

Dr. and Mrs. John M. Gallalee; Major Jack Gallalee; Dr. H. A. Kirksey; Mr. B. B. Comer, Jr.; Mr. H. L. Upshaw; Mrs. Augusta Gillman Bibb; Mrs. S. G. Swain; Montgomery Board of Education; Mrs. Joseph W. Arburthnot, Sr.; Mr. and Mrs. Leroy McEntire; Mrs. J. B. Griffin.

Mrs. James Kenan; Mr. and Mrs. Julian Elliott; Miss Willie Welch; Mrs. Eleanor B. Perdue; Mrs. John Mayo; Mrs. Maude Smith; Mr. J. J. Askins; Mrs. Mary Welch Lee; Mr. Curtis Frizzell; Miss Mary Mullen; Miss Adelaide Rogers.

Mrs. Nathalie Whitfield Winn; Mr. Asa Whitfield; Mrs. Margaret Reynolds Smith; Miss Bayne Gorgas; Mrs. George Palfrey; Mrs. J. P. Burchfield; Miss Bama Watson; W. E. Belcher Lumber Company; Dr. and Mrs. James Kendrick; Mrs. M. G. Kersh; Mrs. S. E. Hodges; and Mrs. Allen M. Pearson.

Special thanks go to Mr. and Mrs. Edward DeVesci of Rosemount for their considerable help and advice; to Mr. and Mrs. Nathaniel Welch for their constant encouragement and support; to Mr. John Hancock, Member, American Institute of Architects, for reading the manuscript; to Mr. Talbot Hamlin, professor of architecture, Columbia University; to the Fine Arts Division, Library of Congress; to the Alabama Department of Archives and History; to the Amelia Gayle Gorgas Library, University of Alabama; and to the Mobile Public Library.

The author is greatly indebted to Mr. Edwin B. Lancaster, Member, American Institute of Architects, who drew the floor plans for the book, and who also read the manuscript.

TABLE OF CONTENTS

CHAPTER IV

CHAPTER V

CHAPTER VI

CHAPTER VII

CHAPTER VIII

CHAPTER I

The Ante-Bellum Mansion Movement in Alabama

Locations of all mansions included in this book

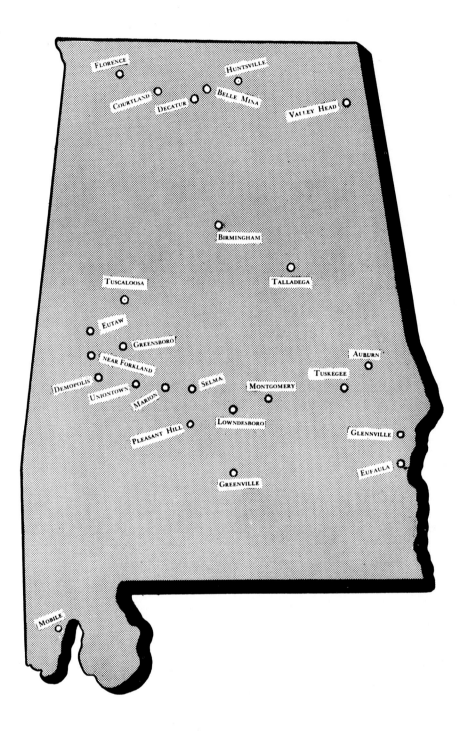

THE ANTE-BELLUM MANSION MOVEMENT IN ALABAMA

Since the beginning of time, buildings have been milestones in the expression of man's ideas. Architecture has been the tool, the instrument with which man has carved many of his finest ideas into permanent man-made structures, many of which are as soaring, as winglike, as monumental, as inspiring as ever to come from the mind of man.

In a material sense, the history of man can be traced by the buildings he has left behind. How richer, how more abundantly complete has been our knowledge of man's historical accomplishments through the discoveries at Pompeii, in the Egyptian tombs and in the excavated structures of the Middle East! From crudely chiseled caves in the early beginning, man has grown so robustly that he has built staggering structures which soar beyond a hundred stories into the sky, and delicate edifices of worship of jewel-like beauty—all of them monuments to his immense achievements attained through the labor of mind and hand.

This book is devoted to that small segment of man's architectural development which occurred in the State of Alabama during the forty year period from 1820 to 1860. During that brief period, time, conditions, and geography were ripe for the sudden development of a mansion building era which had for its goal, unadorned beauty, lasting dignity, boldness toned with grandeur, quality of line and form and grace, magnificence of conception, and a profound goodness and permanence of construction. It was an era in which man strove for beauty in much the same manner as did the ancient Greeks thousands of years ago; an era in which the Alabama builder borrowed much from his Greek predecessor and proceeded then to add his own inspirations and ideas which thus provided buildings that suited his needs, his luxuries, his desires.

From whence did all of this sudden upsurge of beauty arise? What were its roots? Who fathered its infancy? What conditions made it possible?

First of all, one should remember that a building era flourished in Greece and Asia Minor with the development of the Doric order in the 600's B.C. and later tapered off with the perfection of the Corinthian order in Athens as late as 100 B.C. During this 500-year period, great and magnificent temples were erected to the gods worshipped by the people. The finest of these temples were erected in Athens—such temples as the Parthenon, Tower of the Winds, Choragic Monument of Lysicrates, Temple of Nike Apteros, and the Erechtheum, as well as dozens of other almost equally splendidly constructed temples.

However, all of the influence did not spring from the Greeks. The ancient Romans also made contributions, often bolder and cruder, yet retaining a marked degree of high quality. Their civilization centered in Rome where they built such magnificent structures as the Temple of Vesta, the Pantheon, Theatre of Marcellus, Hadrian's Mausoleum and the Baths of Diocletian. However, their work of good architecture extended into the far-flung Roman Empire, notable examples of which can today be seen in the famous baths in Bath, England, and the Maison Carrée in Nîmes, France. To both Julius Caesar and Emperor Augustus must go much of the credit for the fine building era achieved by the Romans. The Romans developed their own versions of the ancient orders of column decorations, adding the Tuscan and Composite to what the Greeks had previously used, namely, the Doric, Ionic and Corinthian orders.

Strangely enough, nearly all of these above mentioned buildings in one way or another made their influence felt in Alabama during the flush times of the ante-bellum building period. Those influences came to life through a variety of factors.

Like so many phases of human growth, the resurgence of the Classic Revival architecture did not begin at any particular date, nor was any one man responsible for its rebirth. Obviously, the flourishing of such a grandiose era of building could come only in a civilization where there existed leisure, luxury, an appreciation of refinement and the beautiful, and, perhaps most important, the wherewithal to make possible such a building development.

Alabama was fast becoming such a place in 1820.

A vibrant love for freedom, newly gained from European dominance, sought means to express itself, not only in buildings, but in the sudden founding of universities; in the beginning of a new culture expressed in fiction, music, poetry and art; and in the founding of newspapers, magazines and publishing houses.

It was only natural that the free people of America should turn to ancient Greece, the country which had long ago lived under a democratic form of government, the country in fact which gave to us the very word democracy: *demo*—people; *kratia*—rule. *Demokratia*—rule of the people.

English and Continental architects began to arrive in America and settle down to serious work, because it was America which at that time offered the fullest building opportunities. A new country was suddenly becoming alive. New states were being formed. New state capitols, courthouses, schools and mansions were needed immediately.

The English poet, Lord George Byron, was instrumental in this turning to Greece for inspiration. Fired with a deep passion for freedom, Lord Byron left his beautiful homeland, as well as his romantic vacation times in Italy, and in 1823 landed in Missolonghi, Greece to join in the struggle for independence which Greece at that time was waging. His landing set off a wave of excitement throughout Europe not unlike that caused by LaFayette's rousing support of the American Revolution when he came bearing the strong arm of French backing. Although he died shortly after arriving in Greece, the fiery passion for liberty on the part of this poet did much to flame the fire of things Greek throughout the New World.

However, Lord Byron's influence was by no means the beginning of this new wave of influence stemming from Greece. Already in the United States it enjoyed a strong foothold, where it had begun to take root soon after the emergence of the nation as a free republic.

To America's great man, Thomas Jefferson, more than to any other, must go the credit as having been the god-father of the Classic Revival building era in this nation. Though not an architect by profession, Jefferson set the building style for the entire country, a style which almost completely dominated the architectural face of America for more than half a century; a style which ranged from the United States Capitol and White House to one room doctors' offices and tiny slave quarters deep in the interior of the nation.

As a student at Williamsburg's College of William and Mary, young Jefferson showed keen interest in the mathematical and mechanical. The quality of his genius can be realized, when it is remembered that by the time Jefferson was nineteen, he was frequently the dinner guest of Virginia's Governor Fauquier, William and Mary's Chancellor George Wythe, and Jefferson's inspired mathematical professor, Dr. William Small. The stories surrounding the camaraderie of this quartet are now famous in history.

Jefferson was admitted to the bar in 1768, and thereupon began a life of monumental service to his country. He was author of the Declaration of Independence, as well as the Statute of Virginia for Religious Freedom. He served in Virginia's House of Burgesses, was Minister Plenipotentiary to France, Secretary of State under President George Washington, Vice President of the United States, and finally, from 1801-09, President of the nation which he had cradled in infancy.

Hence, it can readily be seen that Jefferson served in the very highest positions of influence. His love for good architecture was generous and helpful and he never once let slip through his fingers an opportunity to raise the standards and spread the popularity of the Classic Revival. He wrote the specifications for the United States Capitol and for a "President's House" when a national contest was held to select the designs. He even submitted a plan himself for the President's House, a plan suggested by the Villa Rotunda near Vicenza, Italy, but it was not selected by the judges.

Jefferson had a great love for domes. As a result of this, he was instrumental in shaping the final design of the magnificent dome atop the national capitol.

He designed the Virginia State Capitol, patterning it after the Maison Carrée in Nîmes, France. He concealed a dome within the capitol rotunda which is unseen from the exterior. After visiting Nîmes on one occasion, Jefferson wrote a friend that he gazed "whole hours at the Maison Carrée, like a lover at his mistress."

Jefferson, by far and away, considered the University of Virginia his greatest contribution in the realm of architecture. Having founded the University, he was given free reign in the execution of its design. The University consisted of ten main structures or pavilions, five on the West lawn, and five on the East lawn. Each of these pavilions was designed from classic orders taken from temples of ancient Rome, including the Theatre of Marcellus, Diocletian's Baths, Temple of Fortuna Virilis, and others. A gigantic rotunda was then placed at one far end of these two rows of pavilions. Jefferson made it the most impressive of all, and adapted it from the Pantheon. Jefferson wanted the university buildings not only to inspire the students but also to assist them in learning all the major orders of architecture which he had carefully placed in the decorative details of the pavilions.

Besides his own superb mansion at Monticello, Jefferson also designed a number of other Virginia mansions, including Barboursville, Poplar Forest, Bremo, Edgehill, Farmington and Redlands.

Jefferson was by no means the only person of his day devoted to the Classic Revival. Benjamin Henry Latrobe, who became a close friend of Jefferson, was the first great architect in America who developed the Classic Revival to its fullest possibilities. As Surveyor of Public Buildings under Presidents Jefferson and Madison, Latrobe had a golden opportunity to embody the noblest, the finest of Greek qualities in public buildings being constructed throughout the new nation. Latrobe's outstanding contributions include the United States Capitol, the Bank of Pennsylvania in Philadelphia, the Baltimore Cathedral, the Lousiana Bank in New Orleans, and many others.

Latrobe's contribution to Greek Revival architecture was almost as important in the pupils he taught as in the buildings he designed. The paramount scope, the supreme beauty which he had injected into the buildings he planned was carried forth and enlarged upon by his two prize students, William Strickland and Robert Mills, both of whom have enduring niches of recognition in the field of American architecture.

But, however great may have been the professional abilities of men like Latrobe, Strickland, Mills and others, it was the great classicly minded Jefferson who became the arbiter of fashion for the vigorous new building era sweeping America. His love, his unswerving devotion to beauty, honesty, truth, goodness, purposeful living, joyful creation—all of these spread throughout pioneer America, taking deep root in the minds of people from the Tidewater to the remotest confines of the Louisiana Territory which he purchased.

Is it any wonder then that the greatness of Jefferson should shape itself in the form of hundreds of superbly beautiful mansions and countless public buildings of majestic Greek and Roman Revival design?

Once the national vogue for mansion design had been set, there existed determining factors which made it possible for the mansions in Alabama to begin rising in a still partially Indian inhabited wilderness. These included geography, agriculture, slavery, economics, politics, climate, architects and lay builders.

GEOGRAPHY

Geography had a significant impact upon these mansions. In early Alabama, the white man's civilization largely followed the rivers and wherever rivers ran, there rose stately mansions. So true is this that three-fourths of all the homes included in this volume are on or near rivers. This was inevitable because the only expeditious mode of early travel was via rivers, and too the river systems were the only satisfactory means of transporting King Cotton. Alabama was the perfect state for this river influence to be exercised so fully, in that it has more miles of navigable rivers than any other state in the nation.

While the Tombigbee, Alabama, Tennessee and Chattahoochee were the main rivers traveled, there also were the Cahaba, Tallapoosa, Coosa and Black Warrior. The Tennessee encircles the northern top of the state in the shape of a half-moon, while the great Tombigbee system and the Chattahoochee spread out like a fan, draining the lower extremities of the state. And up and down all of these rivers, the early settlers searched and traveled and sought sites for homesteads, for plantations.

It is an ancient fact that river bottoms are rich lands. (Look, for instance, to the Nile River valley.) The early settlers in Alabama usually were interested in agriculture, and it is only natural that they sought good lands. Knowing that rich top soil continuously is washed into the low-lying river bottom land, the prospective farmers therefore found much of what they were looking for in these river valleys: Easy transportation, rich soil and flat lands.

SLAVERY

Closely coupled with agriculture was the means of production, namely slavery. There could have been no golden era of lavish prosperity for the plantation gentry had it not been for the thousands of slaves who labored as beasts of burden. It was a system based upon the crude and barbaric exploitation of human beings; debasing them and making of them animals to breed, produce, and work, work, work—always work, in order to swell the coffers of the masters.

It was a system founded upon evil; a system void of moral integrity; a system which thinking Americans like Ralph Waldo Emerson fought to abolish many decades before the holocaust of war finally outlawed it.

Slaves represented wealth. Their value ranged usually from five hundred to one thousand dollars. And the man who owned a goodly number held a solid investment. The average planter owned but few slaves, perhaps ten. And even the largest of the plantations seldom had more than fifty; however, a few did have as many as two hundred and fifty. The ownership of slaves has come down to us today as a romantic thing, perhaps because of its connotations of luxury, abundance and prosperity. Hence, many a romantic soul who today tells of the great slave holdings of his ancestors is often found to be living in a realm of traditional hear-say.

While slaves usually assured prosperity, they also had an odious effect upon many an offspring of the original masters. Sons and daughters were reared in such an air of sedate aristocracy that one was not considered a gentleman or a lady who engaged in even the most menial tasks of everyday life. Many ladies became like queen bees, surrounded by workers to answer every beck and call. Usually every child of the wealthiest masters had a personal servant, and many of the mansions had a bell system whereby the inhabitant of each room could call for his personal servant. Each slave knew his call by the tone of the bells, arranged in rows in the servants quarters.

And where for the men could his dependence be more ridiculously exemplified than in their going off to the Civil War, each with his own body servant!

Such complete dependence upon others left a decadent imprint upon the lives of those who had a tendency to be weak. It brought about degeneracy of moral responsibility and a decadent outlook upon life. Thus the slave system which held the seed to the South's golden age was also responsible in many ways for the collapse of that era of luxury and gaiety.

The Civil War itself did not bring complete disaster to all the plantation people. Those who were strong of character and moral fibre returned to their lands and accepted the economic ruin as a challenge and endured bitterly to restore a dignified life for themselves and their descendants. But those who had given in to the softness, the dissipation, the abeyance of responsibility—these were utterly lost and their former way of life was swept from beneath them as suddenly as if a great tidal wave from the Tombigbee or the Tennessee had rolled up and over their lands, carrying away all that stood in its course.

There is here no intent to minimize the almost total economic disaster which befell the plantation life after the Civil War. The ruin was tragic and was soon greatly worsened by the almost illiterate and abominable Reconstruction Era forced upon the loser. Yet despite this tragic era, and despite the torch of Wilson's and Croxton's Raiders whose intent was to fire the buildings of culture—the mansions, the state university, public structures—in much the same manner as Sherman seared the countryside of Georgia, despite all of these, many fine plantation mansions remain intact today due largely to the unstinting determination and belief on the part of the owners that victory could come from defeat. They did the work of former slaves, they labored, they struggled in order to preserve that which they had carved out of a wilderness, as well as to reestablish themselves as independent, self-governing people.

ECONOMICS

Money had much to do with the building of these mansions. The golden era in Alabama was a time of great prosperity. Fortunes were made in a decade, many in less time. Great plantations produced bountiful cotton crops which were hastily shipped to the cotton mills of Manchester and other English cities in the Midlands. Some few planters became such large operators that they owned steamboats for shipping their private cotton crops. Others chartered boats for exclusive trips. It was not unusual for a planter to make as many as five thousand bales of cotton in one year, since a few plantations spread over twelve to fifteen thousand acres. Some of these same plantations have continued to grow and are today even larger in acreage.

Many of the planters brought much capital with them when they came from the Carolinas and Virginia. Nathan Bryan Whitfield was a very wealthy man when he built Gaineswood. Colonel Isaac Croom who built Magnolia Grove was also a man of considerable means, as also were Thomas Bibb, Walker Reynolds, Leroy Pope, Israel Pickens, and others. For these it was easy to double and treble their investments in surprisingly brief years. This wealth enabled the builders to construct dwellings as sumptuous as their hearts desired. Almost for the very first time, houses in America were built in the finest splendor that money could afford. Cost meant nothing to many of these men. They wanted houses superbly designed and superbly built—houses to withstand the ravages of time; houses which provided gracious living and lush comforts.

They built mansions, thinking nothing of spending as many as ten years of laborious effort in perfecting a house which met their every desire. They not only purchased the finest materials and imported the most exquisite of marble mantels, they also sought the services of the few architects who were attracted to Alabama and the South by this challenging new building movement and also by the excellent remunerative gain which the work afforded.

POLITICS

Wherever the political destiny of the state centered, there immediately sprung up many good houses. It was quite natural for people of means to focus their attention upon the state capital. Nowhere is this more clearly seen than in the few brief years in which Cahaba served as the first state capital. Stately houses were built, and then when the capital was moved to Tuscaloosa those same houses were left in a ghostlike atmosphere. And today only one remains in what once was a thriving capital city.

The twenty years, 1826-46, in which the capital was located at Tuscaloosa, saw a mushrooming of magnificent homes in the Classic Revival manner. By the dozens they were built and many remain today as examples of the state's most notable dwellings of the Greek Revival period.

Politics then moved the state capital to Montgomery where a goodly number of fine houses had already been built, but the new state capitol building, dignified and of superb Greek Revival conception, set the fashion for many another white pillared mansion.

Huntsville, of course, cannot be overlooked as a city coming under the sphere of political influence in the building of its homes. It was there that the leaders of the state gathered in 1819 to draw up a constitution and organize a state government. In the early history of the state, Huntsville people played a tremendous role in the affairs of government, with numerous governors making their homes there.

The politics of Spain and France left influences in Mobile, a city founded by the French, and until this day a thriving metropolis which still uses ornamental iron on even its office buildings and its functionalized dwellings. The architecture of Mobile is largely dominated by the ironwork motif. It never felt a full impact of the Classic Revival. Consequently as one browses along Saint Joseph Street, Government Street, Conception Street, Theatre Street, or any one of half a hundred other streets, it is the delicate patterns of iron gates, overhanging balconies, sturdy fences—all of iron—which greet the eye. However, the constant painting and repainting has done much to mar the details of design, which in ante-bellum days were regularly rubbed with stove polish to ward off rust and to give the glow of pride and prosperity.

This widespread use of iron shows further innovation on the part of the mansion builder in Alabama. He was impressed by its beauty, which took the form of patterns highly suggestive of the acanthus scroll or the *fleur-de-lis*. And undoubtedly, too, he was impressed by its durability. Here was decorative building material that could vie with stone and brick in lasting endurance.

The influence and use of ornamental iron spread throughout the state. At least one-half of the Classic Revival mansions pictured in this book contain ironwork balconies. Some of the handsomest of these, such as seen at Mount Ida or the Gillman Home, extend the full length of the veranda.

Often the motif was used even more fully, as in the Gillman Home in which an entire side portico is fashioned completely from exquisite ironwork. The most lavish use of ironwork in upstate Alabama is in the low rambling, French influenced Nunn Home in Autaugaville, where tall stairs, porch balusters, supporting posts, and patterns of fruits and birds-on-wing make for a most spectacular display of ornamental iron almost fairy-like in delicacy and scale.

CLIMATE

Climate had a far reaching effect upon the architecture of Alabama's ante-bellum mansions. Alabama, with a latitude similar to that of Spain and Southern France, enjoys long summers. In Mobile the verandas are commonly used the year round except in January and February. In the Tennessee Valley regions they are used about eight months out of the year. Hence, a lot of living is done on the veranda. The heat of summer becomes intense, and with all the clever attempts to coax the breezes inside the mansions, it is only the shaded porches that give a measure of comforting relief.

It was in the building of the verandas that the masters achieved their most remarkable success. They very ingenuously fitted the architecture to the needs of their daily living. They took the basic designs of orders, columns and pediments from the handbooks of Nicholson and Lafever, and others, and then each added his own whimsical ideas. Great imagination went into the verandas. It was almost as if each builder tried to outdo his plantation neighbor, or the town house builder down the street. One thing they all agreed upon: The veranda was king: Every house, aspiring to be a mansion, must have a veranda. And the products of their imagination are beauties to behold. The lofty magnificence of the veranda at Rosemount; the delicacy and grace of the one at the Bragg Home; the four-sided columned veranda at Forks of Cypress; the ridge-top perch of the one at the Pope Home; the stately dignity of the President's Mansion's veranda at the University, with its double wrought iron stairs spiriling upward to the main floor; and the ambitious and beautifully executed veranda of Winston Place—all of these, and many others, show great freedom of conception, departing widely from the conservative Greek Revival porticoes found along the Atlantic Seaboard and in the Finger Lake region of upstate New York. Builders delighted in this trend of modification and put great enthusiasm into building a veranda different from their neighbors.

Even when engaged in such flights of imaginative fancy, something of the integrity of the builders is indicated by the fact that they never, (or seldom) lost sight of the basic fundamentals of good architecture. They sought always for honesty in their dwellings: no false façades, no shams, no veneered surfaces; all had to be exceedingly strong and had to hue to the most austere disciplines of line, form and order.

And so, the veranda of the Greek Revival era reached its pinnacle in the hands of the architects and builders of the grand manner mansions of Alabama, for nowhere are there verandas which surpass these in scope, massiveness, grandeur, and honesty of the Greek Revival intent and purpose.

Verandas for leisure, verandas for play, verandas for courting—they served multiple purposes and brought comfort and joy to the dwellers of the mansions.

And they were built always with an eye to the weather.

The verandas were not the only feature of these houses influenced by climatic conditions. There was the type dwelling labeled the "raised cottage," a dwelling in which the main part of the house is located on the first floor, over and above the ground floor level. This ground floor is most often used for bedrooms because they are cooler during the hot nights, and also because the first story acts as an insulation for the overhead sun.

Mobile had dozens of these raised cottage dwellings. They are also found infrequently in upstate Alabama, notable examples being the Gorgas Home, Umbria, and the most spectacular example of all, the President's Mansion at the University.

Undoubtedly the climate was the determining factor in the use of the T plan house. The top of the T formed the backside of the house. Bedrooms were built on the pro-

24

jecting ends and ventilation came from three sides, thus making for comfort during the long summer months. Occasionally this plan was inverted with the front of the house forming the top of the T; this plan is frequently found in Tennessee but very seldom in Alabama.

It is much to the credit of these early builders that they considered so wisely the demands of climate, and fitted so well their needs to the weather.

ARCHITECTS

What of the architects who built these houses? Several left a sturdy impact upon the architecture of the state. They built churches, schools, courthouses, but mostly they built mansions: White pillared mansions of the Greek Revival period.

William Nichols, in a smaller degree, did for the University of Alabama what the aged Thomas Jefferson did for the University of Virginia. Jefferson's citadel of learning had been opened to students only five years when the University of Alabama was founded in 1831. However, it was on March 24, 1828 that Nichols first submitted estimates to the state legislature, convened at Tuscaloosa, for the proposed state university. Wtih the money appropriated to commence the building program, Nichols began his work. No doubt he drew heavily from the ideas of Jefferson's quadrangle of buildings. Nichols placed a handsome rotunda at the focal point of the quadrangle. The gem structure of them all, it had three stories, the first two used as an auditorium, and the top floor for the library—the same plan as the rotunda of Jefferson's. Nichols placed twenty-four columns around the Roman type rotunda.

The Gorgas Home was part of the original group of buildings, it being completed in 1829. Nichols also was the architect of the President's Mansion at the University, completed in 1841. It is one of the most skilfully designed mansions in the state. Unfortunately, all of these university buildings, except the Gorgas Home, the President's Mansion and the observatory, were burned by Federal troops during the Civil War.

Nichols was a prolific architect. When the state capital was moved to Tuscaloosa in 1826, he was commissioned to design the capitol building. It too was destroyed by fire, but not until 1923 when it was being used as a female academy. To Nichols also must go credit for the old Mississippi State Capitol at Jackson. He replaced John Lawrence of Nashville when the building, then about one-third finished, was found to have defective conditions, and supervised the project until it was completed in 1839, making many changes in the original plan. Continuing his work in Mississippi, Nichols in 1842 designed the governor's mansion in Jackson. Whether he designed other of the Tuscaloosa mansions is not known, however it is very likely that he did.

Stephen Decatur Button designed the central body of Alabama's elegant Neo-Classic State Capitol in Montgomery, one of the finest Greek Revival public buildings in the entire nation.

Early Huntsville was indeed fortunate in having George Steele as a permanent resident, because he spent the better part of a life time designing beautiful structures there. He designed the Madison County courthouse, with porticoes of the Doric order on all four sides. Feeling undoubtedly that he had to follow the trend of the times, he crowned the structure with a dome, as William Strickland had lately done in building the nearby state capitol at Nashville. However, Steele's dome was insignificant and incongruous with the beauty of the Greek porticoes. His finest public building was Huntsville's First National Bank, still standing, with a superb Greek façade. Five Huntsville mansions which he designed include the Cabaness House, Clay House, Steele-Fowler Mansion, Leroy Pope Home, and it is said by some that he also had a hand in the design of Oak Lawn, however, this has not been confirmed. In all of these structures Steele followed closely the descriptions, delineations and drawings as set forth in the various handbooks of the day. The Greek motif was his forte and he used it wisely and with respect. His skill added greatly to the Alabama heritage of fine architecture.

A ravishing fire destroyed much of Mobile's downtown area in 1827. As a result, a new building era immediately began. The city by now had become a thriving seaport town, with much business and trading being transacted. To accommodate these flush times, there was a demand for public buildings of quality. Some of the nation's finest architects began to arrive from the North.

James and Charles Dakin designed the domical Barton Academy, built in 1835-36. It was the first public school erected in Alabama, and by far the most imposing. It could very fittingly and proudly have served as a state capitol, so magnificent is it. The Dakin brothers also did Government Street Presbyterian Church. It is dated 1837, and remains even until this day, perhaps the most beautiful church in Alabama. Charles Dakin later moved to Mobile and settled down for a life time of work. However, death soon snuffed out his highly promising career.

James Gallier, a former partner of Minard Lefever, first gained southern recognition when he won first prize for designing a proposed city hall for Mobile. However, it was not erected in accordance to his plans. He moved on to New Orleans where he gained fame and fortune from his architectural profession.

The United States Marine Hospital, with its great colonnaded front of sixteen pillars covering the better part of an entire city block, is cautiously attributed to Robert Mills.

Claude Beroujon came from France in 1826 with Right Reverend Michal Portier, the first bishop of Mobile, and designed the massive Cathedral of the Immaculate Conception which was under construction from 1836-50. Beroujon also remodeled and drastically changed the character of the modest dwelling known as the Portier House, the home of the bishop. Beroujon and James Freret designed the main building of Spring Hill College, founded by Bishop Portier in 1830. However, this structure was destroyed by fire in 1869. Freret was from the outstanding family of New Orleans' architects who worked there for four generations. As far as can be established, Spring Hill College is James Freret's only contribution to Mobile architecture.

Thomas Simmons James contributed much toward making Mobile known for its good architecture. In 1855 he did the huge City Hall, with expansive inner courts, great cast-iron gates, and low pedimented façades. He is also recorded as having done the Madame le Vert House, Augustine-Ottenstein House, and the Bragg House, Mobile's finest Greek Revival mansion, as well as the residences of James Battle, Dr. George H. Ketchum and C. K. Foote. It is said that he drew plans for the Richards House. He also worked in Natchez, Jackson and New Orleans.

Peter Hamilton and Erwin Craighead, Mobile's two foremost historians, both claim James as the architect of Barton Academy and Government Street Presbyterian Church.

However, Talbot Hamlin's *Greek Revival Architecture in America,* the most definitive work ever done on the subject, says that James and Charles Dakin were the architects for the two buildings. His information was derived from documents held by the Dakin family which show that the Dakin brothers actually designed the structures in question. Their claim is also substantiated by James Gallier's *Autobiography* published in Paris in 1864.

The Mobile Directory of 1837 lists the following:

"Dakin, Charles B. and James H. Company firm of Dakin & Bros. Architects, office south side Government, 5th from Royal."

It also has the following entry:

"James, T. S., Bricklayer. Office on Government Street below Royal."

Judging from information gathered from the Dakin family documents, it looks as if the Dakin brothers must certainly be credited with both the Barton Academy and Government Street Presbyterian Church.

The Boston architect, Isaiah Rogers, in 1820-21 drew plans for the first theatre ever erected in Mobile.

Henry Moffatt was engaged as architect for Mobile's Protestant Orphans Home at 911 Dauphin Street.

At Martin's Station, just north of the first state capital city of Cahaba, Richard Upjohn designed Saint Luke's Episcopal Church in the Gothic Revival manner. The building was later dismantled and moved to Marion. Upjohn was the noted exponent of Gothic Revival who displayed a delightful and honest balance of design in the many small churches he planned, as well as in such larger religious edifices as Trinity Church in New York City.

B. F. Parsons was the architect of Perry County courthouse in Marion, as well as the designer of Pitts' Folly in Uniontown.

Thomas Helm Lee, a cousin of Robert E. Lee, was commissioned to come to Alabama and design the Parkman-Watts-Gilman Home in Selma, one of the very finest in the state.

General Hiram H. Higgins in 1843-44 designed and built Founders Hall, the main building of Athens College, Athens, Alabama. It is an imposing Greek Revival structure.

In Decatur, James Fennell, not an architect by profession, built the old State Bank in 1832, an exceptionally fine building. The courtyard to the rear is enclosed by a serpentine wall, no doubt inspired by Jefferson's similar walls built only six or seven years previously at the University of Virginia.

It has been reported from more than one source that Benjamin Latrobe, architect of the United States Capitol, was the designer of Carlisle House near Marion. However, this has never been substantiated. Latrobe worked in New Orleans during 1820-21, where he designed the water works building and the Louisiana Bank. It is very unlikely that he provided Edwin K. Carlisle plans for his Gothic mansion, especially so, since Latrobe died in 1821, and Carlisle Hall was not begun until some five years later.

Thus when all the architects who were actually known to have worked in Alabama are assembled as a unit, they comprise a notable group, several of whom were great architects of the Greek Revival and the Gothic Revival periods.

The number of architects who worked in ante-bellum Alabama was small compared with the tremendous demand of the time. There simply were not enough trained professionals to supply the demand. Alabama had suddenly become very prosperous in the 1820's and '30's. It was only natural that planters, rich overnight, should want grand manner mansions to establish them as men of success, esteem and gracious, hospitable living. They wanted only the finest. But scarcity of trained technicians limited the building of good mansions.

It is to be assumed that there would have been a far greater number of good homes had the architects been available. There are today some two thousand antebellum houses in Alabama which border onto being of the mansion type. Many of these were built by plantation owners who had ample means to employ even the most demanding architect. But when none could be hired, they turned to the only other available source: namely themselves. A great many of them did not have the classical training of university life. They had not studied geometry, architecture and mathematics. Therefore they were not skilled and could not build houses of quality design. Instead, by the hundreds they erected two story square houses with a hall down the center, and a tightly contained façade with two closely spaced square posts on either side of the porches, upstairs and down. The doors and windows had crude sashes. Mantels were of plain wood and without a suggestion of design. Imagination was relatively absent. Such was the stereotyped pattern for so many of the state's early houses.

A slightly better group of houses were those built by roving carpenters, often referred to at the time as "peripatetic," due to their ambulatory nature. Their plan was to build a house in a town or on a plantation, then move on elsewhere and seek other commissions. They invariably used a single house pattern and, as a result, there are identical houses built in different sections of the state by the same carpenter.

Yet there were a few planters who became master builders and perfected mansions which even the best architects of the day would well liked to have claimed. Most notable of this group was Nathan Bryan Whitfield, the builder of Gaineswood in Demopolis.

While most of these men knew only rudiments of basic architecture, they had minds of profound inquiry and delved into the task of building a mansion with great enthusiasm, as well, no doubt, as a challenge to their own capabilities. Regardless of however brilliant they might have been, they could never have built the fine mansions they did, had it not been for the handbooks of architecture which began to be printed and distributed around 1800. These books contained entire house plans, measured drawings, exact details of design, and a host of suggestions for the lay builder, as well as for the architect. The handbooks featured the structures of Ancient Greece and Rome. The temples were drawn minutely, and for the purpose of utilizing these very designs for actual buildings. If a man was clever enough, he could take one of these handbooks, master the instructions, and come up with a mansion of amazing beauty.

The handbooks had a great impact upon the architecture of Alabama's Greek Revival era. They set the style, they inspired the architect and the lay builder, they provided fundamental information necessary for the building of a grand manner mansion.

It is known that when Nathan Bryan Whitfield started to build Gaineswood, one of the nation's most elegantly pretentious Greek Revival mansions, he had as his Bible a set of *The Antiquities of Athens* by James Stuart and Nicholas Revett. It was this handbook which set the first fashionable trend toward the Greek Revival as a popular style of architecture. Thomas Jefferson referred to it constantly during his building career. Subsequent architects, including Peter Nicholson, relied heavily on the Stuart and Revett works when they began to draw handbooks of their own.

Whitfield used the handbook masterfully. The Corinthian details of the great drawing room were taken from the Choragic Monument of Lysicrates. The columns in the mistress's bedroom and the summer house were fashioned after those employed in the Tower of the Winds. While more information is available on Whitfield's use of the handbooks, it is safe to say that other master builders also followed closely their instructions. Outstanding among these lay builders in Alabama were Williamson Allen Glover who built Rosemount; Walker Reynolds who built Mount Ida; Jonathan Emmanuel who built Emmanuel House in Mobile. And there were others. Francois Girard built the Girard Double House in Mobile. Thomas Bibb built Belle Mina near Huntsville. James Jackson built Forks of Cypress near Florence. James E. Saunders built Rocky Hill Castle near Courtland. J. Innes Thornton built Thornhill at Watsonia. Colonel Isaac Croom built Magnolia Grove at Greensboro. William Overton Winston built Winston Place at Valley Head.

These men showed unusual native ability. They were able to take the handbooks and use the best they had to offer. Yet it was not merely a copying affair. They frequently showed keen imagination by using the core of the Greek design and then adding their own inspired innovations, often coming up with designs unseen elsewhere. It is greatly to their credit that they used the handbooks almost clay-like in their hands, fashioning that which suited their whims, changing details here, adding characteristics there. It is in this manner that the builders of mansions in Alabama evolved a refreshing development of the Greek forms. The Greek patterns were modified to suit the needs of the pioneer builder, and the mansions took on new beauty, especially in spaciousness of rooms and elaborateness of verandas and winding staircases. Often inspired innovations became highly useful as well as ornamental. For instance, there are the iron foot-rests attached to the veranda columns at Mount Ida. At Forks of Cypress the bottom limestone step at the front porch has carved at either end an Ionic scroll in keeping with the Ionic order of the columns. (This same motif is found at the governor's mansion in Richmond, Virginia.)

These builders did more than follow handbooks. They were often faced with primitive conditions of wilderness life. They nearly always made their own brick, felled timber from their own forests and then sawed it for their houses. Occasionally they used limestone or sandstone. And therein lies one of the finest phases of these old mansions, because the builders so often took what native material they had at hand and proceeded to build their houses accordingly. They fashioned Greek revival mansions from red clay and pine trees, and they did it well.

Often they imported marble mantels, columns, pediments, casings for doors and windows, and ornamental ironwork. Yet some even ventured to make all of these, except ironwork, on the place. Whitfield built lathes and casts for his wood and plaster work and achieved high quality in what he perfected.

These builders frequently had skilled slaves who did much of the detail work.

William Jemison set up an instruction school for his most alert slaves on his plantation near Tuscaloosa. In numerous instances, history records where a slave was freed due to his excellent work on the master's new mansion. Infrequently slaves were brought from far away, as was the case of James Bell who came from Virginia to build the three spiral staircases at the Watkins-Moore-Grayson Home in Huntsville. Skilled plaster workers, too, were often brought from the East to execute the highly ornamental plaster ceiling flowers and cornice trim.

A passage which fits exactly the work of these skilled artisans, reads: ". . . so that under his hands the artisan's labor mingles constant gratifications with its inevitable difficulties, and the product becomes an object of pleased contemplation and pride." It was written by philosopher George Santayana in his *Dominations and Power: Reflections on Liberty, Society, and Government.*

CHAPTER II

The Tennessee Valley Region

Florence

Courtland

Decatur

Belle Mina

Huntsville

Valley Head

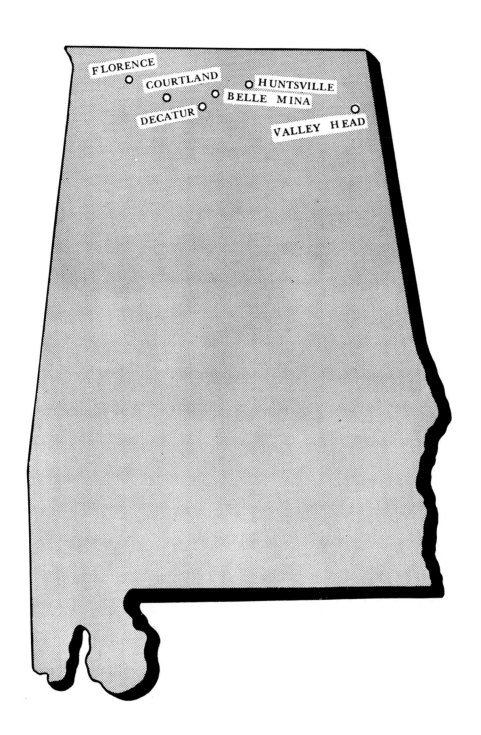

(The Tennessee Valley Region)

FORKS OF CYPRESS, near Florence, Alabama

Alabama's finest example of the temple type mansion, popularized by our most architecturally minded President, Thomas Jefferson, is Forks of Cypress, five miles north of Florence.

This masterfully planned mansion stands like a crown jewel atop a knob-shaped hill, as proudly as if it were one of the great temples which once graced the Acropolis.

Twenty-four towering columns surround the dwelling on all four sides, and give Forks of Cypress the distinction of being the only Greek Revival mansion in Alabama, and one of the few in the entire South, with columns girdling its entirety. Indeed, the columns themselves are the most outstanding feature of the structure. They were hand made on the premises. The bases were hand cut from native stone, and the century-browned columns taper upward to the splendidly proportioned Ionic capitals. Recent repairs reveal that they were made of crossed blocks of wood, overlaid with thick crusts of stucco. Remarkable as it may seem to students of modern construction, this stucco was made by mixing sand, horsehair, and charcoal with molasses. And despite a century of torrid summers and frequent winter snow storms, these molasses-treated columns have stood remarkably well and are today in a sound state of preservation.

The influence of ancient Greece is again in evidence in the craftsmanship of the front steps leading up to the veranda. Flaring out from the ground tier of the steps are hand-cut stone reproductions of the Ionic column capitals.

Atop the columns, the entablature is severely plain and makes for a simplicity of design in keeping with the rest of the house.

The windows, too, follow the simple lines used throughout the mansion. Green blinds on the first floor windows are the only decorations along the wall of wooden siding, other than the fanshaped transom over the double door, bordered on either side by four plain glass panels.

The fact that no denticulation, no pilaster, no window decoration was used, suggests the possibility that Forks of Cypress was built by local artisans and was not under the supervision of one of those skilled artisans who then traveled throughout the South. 1860. Forks of Cypress is definitely a man's house. The entire conception of the exterior suggests an air of boldness and masculinity.

However, the interior has many features of architectural refinement. One enters a T-shaped hall from the front approach, to peer through a broad arch into the wide end of the hall, measuring 23 by 16 feet. Beyond this lies another double door, similar to the one at the front, except here a simple, square paned transom is employed. The mouldings and pilasters used in the parlors and dining hall are of unusual delicacy, all fluted and geared to classic designs. The parlor mantel is hand-carved while the dining room boasts an Adamlike mantel with many hand-carved rosettes.

Upstairs are four great bedrooms, two on either side of the hall. The two largest of these measure 24 feet square. Originally, one was the boys' room and the other the girls' room, and each had four massive four-postered beds to accommodate the overflow of children who were always finding their way to Forks of Cypress and its abounding hospitality.

One of the unique features of the mansion is its air-conditioned basement. Called a 'cellar' in its early days, the basement was dug out of the ground beneath the house. Twelve-inch slit openings give ventilation from beneath each window across the front veranda; and since the top of the basement is lower than the top level of the brick porch, small slits a foot deep and a foot wide run the width of each window and give light and air to the cellar below. The walls around these slit openings were cut from limestone, with notched-out grooves at all corners, each dovetailing into the other and interlocking with a remarkable evenness. In the cellar still remains the great cypress log with its hollowed-out vat-like sections which was used for water storage. The cellar itself was used for storing food, because here it was cool in the summer and warm in winter.

Forks of Cypress was built by an Irishman, James Jackson, who selected the site of his home even before Alabama became a state. He was one of the most romantic figures ever to pioneer beyond the Blue Ridge Mountains. The Cypress Land Company which he helped organize, platted what is today the city of Florence while it was still a forest. The sale of this land marks the most successful early land sale ever staged in Alabama. It brought a rush of people into the Tennessee Valley, and a new way of life soon replaced the crude Indian civilization which had thrived along the river banks.

It was during these robust days that James Jackson built Forks of Cypress on an extensive plantation five miles out of Florence. Big Cypress and Little Cypress creeks border the plantation and merge just beyond the entrance of the half-mile long driveway leading to the mansion located in the forks—hence, Forks of Cypress. The home was built on the commanding spot where once stood the wigwam of Double Head, famed chieftain of the Cherokees.

For many years James Jackson and his beautiful wife, Sally Moore McCullough Jackson, lived a Utopianlike life at The Forks and reared a houseful of children in the aristocratic manner of the Old South. The children were taught music and etiquette by polished governesses, and they read the classics widely. Four times yearly a big box of the newest books arrived from a book dealer in Philadelphia.

James Jackson was a great lover of race horses. He built stables and bred thoroughbreds at The Forks which became national racing champions. A regulation racetrack in the flat meadow in front of the mansion, became the scene of many exciting races.

Jackson would have nothing but the finest of horses, so it was not surprising when he sent a buyer to England in 1835 and purchased Glencoe, once owned by King George IV. Turf histories record Glencoe as being one of the finest horses of all time. Ten years later, Peytona, an off-spring of Glencoe, raced and won before 120,000 spectators—the largest number ever to attend a race in the United States, up to that time. The scene was the Union Course in New York City, and the sporting paper which wrote up the race said, "This was the most gallantly contested as well as the most beautiful race ever seen in this country."

34

James Jackson died in 1840 but his wife kept the plantation going, even after the horses and the slaves went with the Civil War. She lived to be ninety years old and left more than 100 living descendants. One of her great-great-grandsons, David Milton, married Abbie, daughter of John D. Rockefeller.

Today, James Jackson, his wife, Sally, and many of his descendants sleep in the family burial ground to the back of the house. And so, the master of Forks of Cypress rests on the ground he cherished most dearly of all—there within sound of the galloping hoofs which once raced like the champions they were.

The Forks is now owned by Mr. R. B. Dowdy of Montgomery.

Forks of Cypress has twenty-four columns. It is Alabama's only ante-bellum mansion with a colonnaded veranda extending around all four sides of the dwelling.

Forks of Cypress. The originality of the builder is shown in the Ionic motif cut into the bottom slab of the front steps.

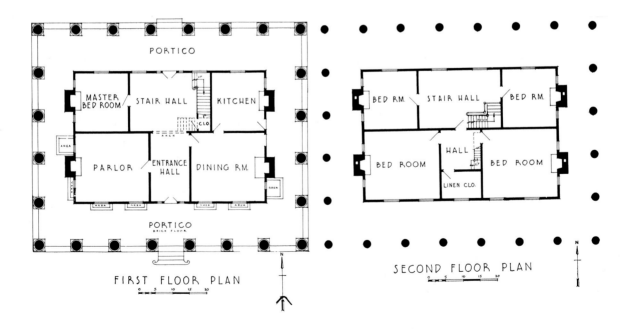

36

THE FOSTER HOME: COURTVIEW, Florence, Alabama

Nothing short of a special act of the Alabama legislature was necessary for the building of the Foster Home in Florence. Court Street is the thoroughfare which rises from the banks of the Tennessee River and extends through the heart of the city. So when George Washington Foster, wealthy planter, desired to erect a mansion at the top and in the center of the thoroughfare, he had to petition the legislature for authority to close off the street and build flanking avenues along either side of the estate. Foster was voted permission on the condition that the house he built should be of such beauty that it would justify the inconveniences caused the people of the city.

Florence was already a thriving town when Courtview was built. The date is apparently fixed by the following inscription which in recent years was found on the trolley of the sliding parlor doors: "John Ballinger, carpenter and builder, Aug. 24, 1855."

Florence itself had its birth, March 12, 1818, when a group of industrious settlers met in Huntsville and organized the Cypress Land Company. They purchased 5,515 acres from the government for the sum of $85,235.24. The tract extended from Campbell's Ferry to the confluence of the Tennessee River and Cypress Creek, all of which was on the north side of the Tennessee. The charter which they drew up said that they represented an "association of respectable, opulent and enterprising individuals." Leaders in the movement were General John Coffee, hero of the Battle of New Orleans and surveyor general of the Alabama Territory, and James Jackson, builder of Forks of Cypress and rich horse-racing promoter and enthusiast. Stockholders also included Thomas Bibb, Leroy Pope, and United States Supreme Court Justice, John McKinley. Lots were sold to such renowned statesmen as former President James Madison, President James Monroe, and President-to-be Andrew Jackson. Money received from the colorful land sale totaled the dazzling sum of $319,513.00, a neat profit indeed.

Florence is probably the only city in Alabama which had an over-all plan from its very inception. The founding fathers employed the services of a young Italian surveyor and designer named Ferdinand Sanona to shape a city plan and lay it out accordingly. Having grown up in Florence, Italy, Sanona asked the privilege of naming the new Alabama city after his own beloved Florence. It was at the head of the main street in this beautifully planned town that George Washington Foster built his Greek Revival mansion.

Courtview is a fine example of the very best of the new classical building order. Here the styling is compact, held severely to the formal Greek concept. There is no lavish veranda, no innovations, no far-flung additions. The four distinguished fluted Ionic columns, enhanced by a touch of the egg-and-dart pattern, are compactly aligned on a portico of almost Georgian dimension. And crowning the otherwise Greek unity of the whole portico is a refined and graceful use of the ante-fix around the very topmost edge of the entablature roof. Here is found the finest use of the ante-fix in the state. And to the broad entablature, as well as to the entire eaves of the house, is applied a diminutive dentil design, rectangular in shape.

Courtview has three stories. The top two are made of brick, earth brown in color, said to have been made by slaves, while the ground floor and steps are constructed of stone slabs. Heavy iron grillework borders the balcony and the narrow porch below.

Inside, the floor plan follows the traditional scheme. A large hall extends through the middle, with a parlor and music room to the right, and the dining room, kitchen and a bedroom to the left. The two front rooms, the parlor and the dining room, each have two windows which open as doors onto the gallery.

The parlor and music room have a broad wooden cornice with a center strip, beaded at top, of scrolled leaves and fruit carved in wood. The two rooms also have an Italian influenced medallion of scrolled acanthus leaves, centered with four clusters of olives on leafy branches, from which hang crystal chandeliers added at a much later date. The entrance hall has a cornice featuring the oak leaf and acorn. The central staircase rises from the middle of the hall and divides in half at the landing to form a double passage—this too was not part of the original construction and does not have the classical elegance found in so many features of the house.

The upstairs floor plan is essentially the same as the first, the chambers being bedrooms.

The house passed from the builder to his daughter, Sallie Foster McDonald, wife of S. P. McDonald, captain in the Confederate Army. Then in 1900 it became the home of Governor Emmett O'Neil of the famous father-son governor combination, his father, Edward A. O'Neil having been elected governor in 1882. In 1922 it passed to the Thomas Rogers family, and it was they who added the hall stairs and lovely chandeliers tailored for the particular rooms. The mansion is now the property of the Florence State Teachers College, which adjoins it to the rear. It is used as a student and faculty social center. The ground floor has been made into a museum, possessing many historic items and rare relics.

The profusion of old-fashioned boxwood in the front lawn forms a great heart shaped design, suggesting the intricate pattern work of the formal English gardens.

It seems entirely befitting that this very handsome mansion is now a public building, and that its many architectural delights can be enjoyed by so many.

Foster Home: Courtview. The parlor and music room have Italian medallions with scrolled acanthus leaves and clusters of olives on leafy branches.

Foster Home: Courtview. George Washington Foster was a man of great wealth, but it took an act of the Alabama legislature to build his white pillared mansion.

Foster Home: Courtview. Superb Ionic columns and the queenlike, crowning touch of the antefix are framed here by spruce and magnolia.

40

Foster Home: Courtview. The marble mantel in the parlor is severely plain.

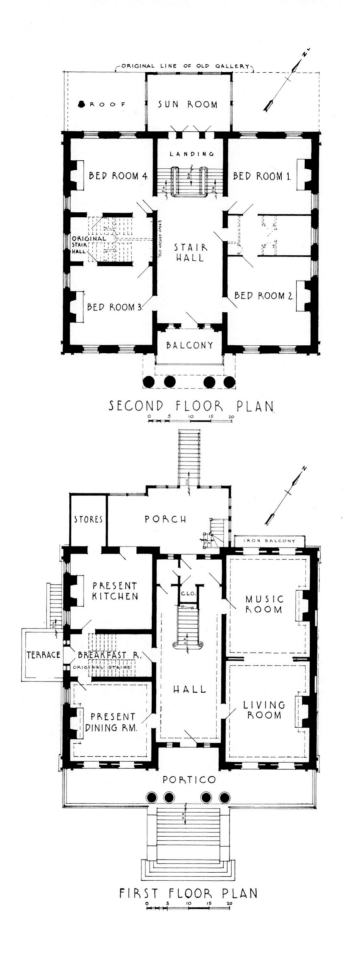

ORIGINAL LINE OF OLD GALLERY

ROOF

SUN ROOM

LANDING

BED ROOM 4

BED ROOM 1.

ORIGINAL STAIR HALL

OLD ARCHED OPEN'G

STAIR HALL

BED ROOM 3.

BED ROOM 2.

BALCONY

SECOND FLOOR PLAN

0 5 10 15 20

PORCH

STORES

IRON BALCONY

PRESENT KITCHEN

CLO.

MUSIC ROOM

TERRACE

BREAKFAST R.

ORIGINAL STAIRS

HALL

PRESENT DINING RM.

LIVING ROOM

PORTICO

FIRST FLOOR PLAN

0 5 10 15 20

ROCKY HILL CASTLE, Courtland, Alabama

More than a few of the notable mansions up and down the Tennessee River valley had the torch put to them by Union troops during the Civil War. Luckily, Rocky Hill Castle was spared such a disaster. It was built by James Edmonds Saunders who was born May 7, 1806 in Brunswick County, Virginia. Saunders, while only eighteen, withdrew from the University of Georgia after marrying beautiful Mary Watkins, fifteen—she being a sister of Sara Independence Watkins, who married George Washington Foster, the builder of Foster Home in Florence.

Saunders, being interested in law, took his bride and went to Nashville, Tennessee, where he entered the firm of Foster and Fogg. Then at twenty-one, he began his own practice in Alabama—first in Moulton, then in Courtland, one of Alabama's oldest towns. It was in Courtland that the first Alabama novel "The Lost virgin of the South," by M. Smith, using the *nom de plume* of Don Pedro Casender was published in 1832. It was dedicated to "Andrew Jackson, President of the 24 United States of America." It was also from the small town of Courtland that Dr. Shackleford marshalled his gallant Alabama Red Rovers for the Mexican War, every last one of whom, except the medical staff of eight, were shot to death by the Mexicans.

So James Edmonds Saunders picked a thriving locality when he chose to settle in Courtland on Big Nance Creek. Saunders entered public life early and was elected to the state legislature in 1835, while only twenty-nine. Later he lived temporarily in Mobile where he was customs collector for the Port of Mobile. He was a member of the electoral college during both the James K. Polk and the Franklin Pierce elections. In the meantime, he also had been made a trustee of the University of Alabama.

His political pre-eminence led to his election as president of the Stephen A. Douglass Convention which convened in Montgomery, Alabama, 1860, in an effort to avert the horrors of war which hovered so near. Saunders, like many another plantation owner, was a strong anti-secessionist and worked devotedly to keep the South from seceding from the Union. But once the grave decision was made, he joined ranks with the Confederate government and rendered distinguished service. He went with his three sons into the Southern Army. As a colonel, he was a staff officer to General Nathan Bedford Forrest. During the battle of Murfreesboro, Tennessee, he was severely wounded, but overcame the wound and lived to be ninety years old.

The exact building date of Rocky Hill Castle is not known. However, it was probably built during the late '40's or early '50's.

The visitor is immediately struck by the odd Gothic tower with supporting wall adjoining the house. With its old world architecture of cold, warlike atmosphere, it is indeed a strange auxiliary for the Greek type mansion. The brick tower with turrets has six floors and was used as a lookout post by the master as he surveyed his vast domain of fields being worked by slaves. The winding steps inside have since disappeared.

The mansion is largely of Greek character. Its almost identical one-story porticoes both to the front and rear are excellent Greek Revival, with an exquisite cornice of the triglyph motif adorning the four fluted Doric columns. Wings added to either side also have small porticoes with two columns each. A profusion of cornice brackets buttresses the overhanging eaves of the roof, and a cupola with arched windows is placed atop the roof. The house is built of brick, plastered over with stucco.

Its exterior could never compete with the loveliness of the interior. The spiral staircase in the entrance hall is a commanding, majestic thing to behold: Spiraling down, it sweeps out wide in a curving manner, leaving the treads gradually broader at the bottom. Then at the crest of the spiral, the banister sweeps around forming a crown of architectural grandeur and sheer loveliness. Great individuality!

Another exceptional use of skill is evident in the massive arched entrance leading from the vestibule into the parlor. The ends of the broad arch rest upon two pilasters, pilasters which appear to be standing on a base carved in the shape of a vase with out-furled acanthus leaves. The panels in the sliding doors are also arched. The chandelier medallion features acanthus leaves. The plaster cornice, done in relief, is very ornate, yet in keeping with the general decor.

A Welsh carpenter named Hugh Jones had a decisive hand in the building of Rocky Hill Castle. It was he who set the pattern for the details. He carved the pilasters, designed the arches, and executed the staircase. He also built the Gothic tower according to instructions from Colonel Saunders, finishing it about the time the war started. He remained at Rocky Hill Castle during the war and died there before it ended.

During the course of the war many notables were entertained at the mansion. On one occasion the Military Court of the Army of Tennessee held a meeting there. Its members consisted of the following: Colonel William H. Saunders, brother of the builder; Judge John Sale of Aberdeen, Mississippi; Colonel William Dowd; and the learned educator, J. L. M. Curry of Talladega, Alabama, later Minister to Spain.

General Pierre Beauregard and his staff dined there once, and a staff member, Colonel William Brent, later became the father-in-law of one of the young Saunders girls.

Thus one can readily see that the comings and goings of the war made opportune background when Ellen Virginia Saunders, who married Judge L. B. McFarland of Memphis, Tennessee, decided to write a novel called "The Little Rebel" which swept the nation and was made into a motion picture.

With the war went Colonel Saunders' fortune, but he stayed on at the plantation, tried his hand at many ventures, including vineyard growing. The golden days were gone, but the family, now with many grandchildren, maintained its dignity, its honor, through the Reconstruction Period. Then in 1874 the master and his wife celebrated their golden wedding anniversary.

Rocky Hill Castle has since gone from the Saunders family. Today its once fabulous furnishings are no longer there. The house itself is empty and beginning to decay. The grounds are closed, the gates locked, and 'No Trespassing' signs posted. But who knows —perhaps tomorrow will again bring the laughter of children, the care of loving hands to Rocky Hill Castle.

Rocky Hill Castle. A vibrant family life and a colorful war atmosphere here formed the background for "The Little Rebel," written by one of its daughters.

BURLESON-HINDS-McENTIRE HOME, Decatur, Alabama

The Burleson-Hinds-McEntire Home in Decatur is so steeped in Civil War history that it might well be called Alabama's most historic house. It was here that Confederate General Albert Sidney Johnston and his staff planned the Battle of Shiloh, April 4, 1862. Following the fall of Vicksburg, Federal Generals Grant, Sherman and Blair met here in 1863 for a war conference. In the spring of 1864 it was used as a headquarters for Federal General G. M. Dodge.

A rare photograph now hangs in the central hall of the mansion which shows the band of the 102nd Ohio Regiment, gathered on the roof of the house, playing a funeral dirge in tribute to President Abraham Lincoln who had just been assassinated.

The house, built sometime during the five-year interval between 1825-30 by John Burleson, overlooks the broad waters of the Tennessee River. A Northerner, Jerome J. Hinds, bought the estate shortly after the close of the war. His brother, Joseph M. Hinds settled in Alabama and lived in the mansion. In 1872 Joseph M. Hinds was appointed consul general to Brazil and Argentina. In Buenos Aires his beautiful daughter, Grace, became the toast of society, and soon married Alfred Duggan, a Tennessee boy who had gone to South America to amass a fortune. Years later, after her husband's death, Grace Duggan married Lord Curzon of England, and became Lady Curzon, Marchioness of Kedleston.

Lord Curzon became Prime Minister of England, and also served as Foreign Secretary to the British Government, and Viceroy of India.

During the years in which her husband served in honored positions, Lady Curzon was noted for her culture, erudition and charm—the latter quality no doubt being largely the result of her rearing in the Decatur, Alabama, mansion where she learned the social graces during a happy childhood and youth.

The house was purchased in 1898 by the McEntire family and it is now the residence of Mr. and Mrs. Leroy McEntire. It is one of the few grand manner mansions in Alabama in which the builder preferred the square pillars to the predominantly popular round columns. The iron fence guarding the two-acre lawn is shown in old Civil War photographs with army blankets flung over it, and apparently was erected shortly after the house was built.

Slum quarters of the city have almost surrounded the historic mansion, but it still is very much a home of culture and hospitality. And the picturesque Tennessee River flows majestically along; a masterpiece of natural beauty as one looks down from the mansion veranda.

Burleson-Hinds-McEntire Home. The saddest moment in the life of this home occurred when the 102nd Ohio Regimental band played a mournful dirge in tribute to Abraham Lincoln, who had just been assassinated.

BELLE MINA, Belle Mina, Alabama

"Thomas Bibb—1826"

These are the words, hand-tooled upon the brass knocker, which greet you even today as you call at the transom-lighted door of Belle Mina, the plantation home of Thomas Bibb.

And a baby's footprint also welcomes you. The builder of Belle Mina took his baby girl, Eliza, to the kiln on nearby Limestone Creek where slaves were making the brick, and upon one of the soft red squares was imprinted the outline of her foot. The brick was then placed in the porch floor directly in front of the main entrance. This very human episode must have given the father much joy as years later he showed the impression to visitors.

Thomas Bibb came from one of Alabama's great families—the one which more than any other shaped the early destinies of the state. Elected presiding officer of Alabama's first senate, which was organized at Huntsville in 1819, Thomas Bibb automatically became governor when his brother, William Wyatt Bibb, was thrown from a horse at Coosada and killed, only eight months after he had become Alabama's first governor.

Even though the new state capital was at distant Cahaba in the south central part of the state, Bibb spent much of his time on his great 2,500 acre plantation of rich red clay land at Belle Mina in Limestone County.

Bibb was born in Amelia County, Virginia, in 1783, and made his first trip to the Tennessee Valley in 1808, via Mobile and the inland river transportation system. The pioneer region appealed to him greatly and he soon returned to Alabama and bought plantation land other than that at Belle Mina, but the latter he was forever to call home. He is recorded in history as the largest pioneer land owner in all north Alabama.

Bibb was two years building his grand mansion which was in keeping with his social, political and economic status. He approached the task with perseverance, improvising and changing plans wherever materials demanded, though never at a sacrifice of quality workmanship. Bibb knew that there was no sawed wood, no ready made brick, no skilled artisans on hand. These handicaps he faced with the same determination as he did the task of making Alabama into a state to take its place alongside Georgia, Tennessee and the Carolinas. He set about building a sawmill, a brick kiln, and carefully searched the slave markets until he found a highly skilled mason to oversee the brickmaking—years later in his will Bibb mentioned this slave mason as possessing valuable skills—and an expert carpenter to supervise the sawing and cutting. But Bibb himself was the coordinator, the man with the ideas.

It is interesting to note that so many of the slaves were trained in the artistic manner. As is pointed out elsewhere in this book, some of them built spiral staircases which until this day draw admiration from designers and architects.

Bricks were made by the tens of thousands. The walls of the house are three feet thick. Then there were the slave quarters, the kitchen and numerous auxiliary buildings and sheds. But probably more bricks than everywhere else combined, went into the building of the massive wall, six feet high, around the entire two-acre tract where the mansion and garden stand. During the Civil War, Federal troops who were camped nearby, used a portion of the bricks from the wall for building purposes. Then when peace came, the Bibb's gave what remained to hard pressed neighbors for the building of homes.

With customary precision, he built the mansion on a rising hillock in the dead-center of his plantation, and it is said that the land extended one mile in every direction. Bibb was master of all his eyes beheld. He had already accumulated a fortune, as well as a family of nine children, when he moved into his new mansion. It is a house which hews severely to the simplicity of the Doric order. And it might be noted here that the Tennessee Valley mansions built in the 1820's follow more closely the Jeffersonian advocated Doric and Ionic orders, than the mansions which were built during the two following decades in central Alabama, where much of the Corinthian and Composite is to be found.

The six great Doric columns are said to have been made each from a poplar log, surrounded with specially designed brick, and plastered. Adding further to their magnificence is the spacing. The span between the two center columns is wider than between the others, thus making a broader opening for the handsome entrance.

The entablature, too, is severely plain, and the hipped roof above drops pleasingly and not too abruptly to the front. Windows across the entire portico are rigidly plain and without overhead decoration—all harmonious with the entire Doric unity. Only the doorway, with its leaded sidelights and sunburst transom, offers a delicacy which suggests the elaborateness that lies within.

Not until 1941, when it was purchased by Dr. and Mrs. Berthold Kennedy, did Belle Mina leave ownership of the Thomas Bibb family. By then the once proud mansion had suffered greatly from the wear of time and the weather and the neglect of upkeep.

But the Kennedys have done nothing short of a miraculous job of restoration and repair. Ceilings were lowered for easier heating, as well as to hide the newly added plumbing and lighting fixtures installed for modern convenience. Rooms and halls were painted and papered throughout; floors were refinished, and furniture of the period and of exceptional quality and refinement was moved in. Much of the antique furniture had been in the New York apartment of the Kennedys, Mrs. Kennedy having been an ardent antique collector for years. Belle Mina is today one of the most beautifully furnished ante-bellum mansions in all Alabama. Every piece of furniture and every item of decoration, whether it be sets of prismatic lusters, Victorian sofas, or candelabra, seems to fit exactly where it is placed.

The library is one of the few paneled rooms in the state. Painted a soft sea green, it is indicative of the culture and refinement which Thomas Bibb brought with the years to Belle Mina.

The chandeliers throughout the house add a lustrous, sparkling finish to the entire appointment. The spiral staircase of carved cherry wood is of major interest. A fan-lighted transom over the door leading into the garden, brightens the rear of the great hall.

Belle Mina is one of the state's very finest plantation-type mansions. Regrettably though, its statesman builder was to live there but thirteen years. He died September 20, 1839—age 56, ending what might have been many more years of useful and worthy service to his family and his state. He was buried in the family cemetery on the plantation, but twenty years later was moved to the Bibb plot in Huntsville's Maple Hill Cemetery, where he rests near four other Alabama governors: Clement C. Clay, Samuel Moore, Reuben Chapman, and David P. Lewis.

Belle Mina, built in 1826 by Thomas Bibb, Alabama's second governor, is a plantation mansion of unusual quality and refinement. It came strongly under the influence of the Classic Revival as popularized by Thomas Jefferson.

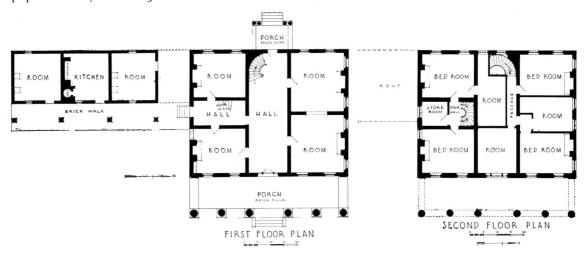

Belle Mina. The spiral staircase, in the entrance hall of ballroom dimensions, has a most graceful sweep.

Belle Mina. The twin parlors are furnished in choice antiques. However, the wooden mantels are the center of attraction. The one shown here is reeded, beaded and fluted, making it, no doubt, the most beautiful wooden mantel used in early Alabama mansion building.

THE POPE HOME, Huntsville, Alabama

The phenomenal blowing spring that gushes forth 24,000,000 gallons of water daily was the attraction which brought settlers early to Huntsville.

John Hunt, pioneer, settled the town in 1805. Land speculators rushed in. Martin Beatty purchased 1,000 acres which included the big spring for the sum of $1,000.00. Four years later this same tract of land was bought by Leroy Pope for $23,000.00. It included what is now practically all of down-town Huntsville, and it is said to have "reached from the big spring to the mountain." Pope named the settlement Twickenham, honoring the British home city of the popular writer of the time, Alexander Pope. But in 1811, when feelings ran hot against the British during the impending War of 1812, the name was changed to Huntsville, for its founder.

Leroy Pope is known as "The Father of Huntsville." He was the pioneer leader who did most to further and encourage growth, stability and progress for the new frontier town, the first settled by white men north of the Tennessee River in what is now the State of Alabama. The town was soon to become the county seat of Madison County which had been organized, December 13, 1808, by Governor Robert Williams of the Mississippi Territory, eleven years before Alabama became a state.

In later years local write-ups have described Huntsville as "the second most healthful city in the United States." However, no sources are listed, nor is the first most healthful city named. This seems to be partially substantiated though by the fact that during the Spanish-American War the area was selected as a rest and medical center for ailing troops.

Leroy Pope lost no time in erecting for himself and his family one of the most magnificent mansions of the entire Tennessee Valley region, and by far and away the finest of its time. He wanted nothing but the very best for his beautiful wife, the former Judith Sale, granddaughter of Captain John Sale who served under General George Washington during the Revolutionary War, and who took charge of the Hessian troops captured during the Battle of Trenton.

In building his mansion, Pope had the services of George Steele, a prominent architect who left a lasting imprint upon the architectural life of Huntsville. It was Steele who set the pattern for the Greek Revival influence in the Huntsville area. Among the finest of his buildings which still stand, are the Madison County courthouse with its superbly designed porticoes on all four sides, the First National Bank, the Cabaness House, the Clay House, his own home known as the Steele-Fowler Mansion, as well as a number of other handsome structures. As a Huntsville resident, Steele did more to further Greek Revival than any other single person in all north Alabama. His life work and influence would make an interesting study for anyone inclined toward the historical approach to architecture.

The Pope Home is built atop Echols Hill, the highest point overlooking the entire city. Its extensive grounds and the bluff beyond the western approach included many acres. The estate has since been reduced, but the grounds are still broad and in keeping with the house which they surround. That house is today Alabama's most photogenic mansion, and certainly one of its most photographed. It was built around 1815. Since the place was constructed when Huntsville was hardly more than a frontier village, the brick were made in Tennessee and not on the spot, as was so often the case during the two or three decades which followed. Edward C. Betts in his *Early History of Huntsville, Alabama,* states that the bricks for the house were "shipped on flat boats down the Tennessee River to Ditto's Landing, from whence they were hauled to Huntsville."

While the mansion appears most ostentatious from the outside, one has the feeling that Pope built strictly for comfort inside. The rooms, even the parlor, are ordinary in size—none of the elaborate ballroom dimensions here. The windows too are small and do not extend to the floor and open full like a door onto the gallery as was the style with so many mansions of the time. Here again are found the immensely thick walls—due no doubt to the accessibility of brick. This general compactness makes for easy heating during the four or five cold winter months in north Alabama, and also for a pleasant coolness during the extreme summer heat. The brick walls serve as a neutralizing effect for both seasons.

The decorative woodwork of the ceiling is morticed and pinned with pegs and cut nails, indicating excellent carpentry. The floor joists are hand-hewn poplar. The pine flooring, still beautiful and solid, is made of random widths.

It is the portico--a thing of beauty to behold—that gives the Pope Home its crowning effect of architectural delight. There is a lavish use of design, yet all is applied with such dignity and reserve that one is immediately struck with its grandeur as well as its solemnity. The windows aligning the portico are small with simple stone lintels, but the doorhead is elaborate in its delicately graduated shelving effect, suggestive of the Regency. The fanlike transom traditionally found over the entrance is cleverly reserved here for the pediment over the six fine Doric columns, making for perhaps the most unusual pedimental effect to be found in the entire state. The entablature adheres further to this fanshape pattern. Fluted panels of sunburst design are placed between each column and at either end. So here, instead of the decorative emphasis being on the columns and windows, it is placed in the pediment, on the entablature, and the doorhead—a deviation, but a handsome one.

The sunken gardens which once beautified the rear of the estate are no longer there.

Leroy Pope died in 1844, years before his grandson, Leroy Pope Walker, was to become the first secretary of war for the Confederate government. It was this grandson who called the first shot of the Civil War: he ordered Fort Sumter fired upon. The day he issued the order, he made a public address in Montgomery, Alabama, in which he told the people that the cities of New York and Boston would soon fall before the Confederate Navy. He was widely criticized in the South as well as in the North for such boastfulness.

After Pope's death, the mansion was bought by Dr. Charles Patton, and it has remained in his family ever since, having been for many years the Spraggins Home, and now it is in possession of Mr. and Mrs. James F. Watts—the descent being through the filial side of the families.

Pope Home. It is the portico that gives this home its crowning effect of architectural delight.

THE WATKINS HOUSE, Huntsville, Alabama

Even though Huntsville was half a century old and already noted for its fine mansions when Robert Watkins, Jr. erected his home in the 1850's, it immediately took its rightful place as a gem in an already gem studded crown.

Like many another early mansion, it was presented by the builder to his queenly bride, Margaret Carter Watkins, who later died from the birth of their seventh child. However, during her lifetime the home was a center of hospitality, much entertainment, and the laughter of romping children.

With the exception of Gaineswood, the Watkins House possesses the finest interior of any ante-bellum mansion in the state. It is so masterfully designed and executed that when the visitor enters its grand reception hall and looks into the fabulous double parlors, he is greeted by a magnificence of beauty which is lavish in detail, carpentry, plaster work, appointment and charm. Superb is hardly the word for it.

The hall cornice is handsomely trimmed with a compound serpentine moulding three feet in width, perhaps as fine as can be found anywhere. A bronze French chandelier hangs from an acanthus leaf medallion. But it is the perfection of the winding stairs, with its spiral fluted mahogany newel post, that dominates the hall.

Mr. Watkins, ingenious man indeed, was not satisfied with one spiral staircase. A second one, almost equally as beautiful graces the upstairs hall. But it is the third one, extending up to the cupola, which is perhaps the most interesting architecturally. Of fine mahogany, it is smaller and cylindrical and winds around a central shaft into the cupola. From the cupola windows, one can see across all Huntsville and beyond to the river bottom plantation lands.

All three of the stairs were executed by Charles Bell, a Charlottsville, Virginia Negro noted for his ability to create handsome staircases. He traveled down from Virginia especially to do the job, which took three years of his time. And it was a South Carolina Negro artisan who did the elaborate plaster work throughout the house.

The four major doors opening into the first floor hall have raised side and overhead paneling—simple in line and form—extending through the three-foot walls.

Perhaps the only point of regret about the entire interior is that the natural beauty of the superb woodwork has been hidden by white paint. However, one can visualize the richness of the walnut and mahogany.

The double parlors breathe an air of loveliness, gleaned from perfection of detail and artistic display embodied in the exquisite furnishings. Unlike the hall design, the broad parlor mouldings of tiered wood are decorated with a five-inch center strip of grape clusters and scrolled leaves, cast interchangeably in plaster. Centering the ceiling of each parlor is an elaborate oval plaster medallion with rings of outfurled thistle leaves, and at either end of each medallion is placed a cherub head, smiling down upon the parlor. The gilt chandeliers are French bronze, featuring the Three Graces, each topped with the heads of three cherubs, similar to those on the medallions overhead.

Each parlor has a satin finish marble mantel, lavish in carved roses and a mixture of flowers, all protruding in relief from the body of the mantel.

The principle furniture in the parlors is a seven-piece set made two decades before the Civil War by the renowned German immigrant craftsman, John Henry Belter. The fanciful carving of fruits and flowers on the two sofas and five chairs is made from numerous thin layers of pressed rosewood. Belter found that this technique gave lasting durability to the rich finesse of his carvings. The set is covered in apple green satin.

The dining room, just beyond the second parlor, with its grey marble mantel, is furnished with an early Empire mahogany banquet set, with an exceptionally fine buffet and glass-fronted china cabinet, all bearing claw-footed legs. A fine ancestral portrait lends dignity and friendliness to the room.

In all, there are sixteen rooms in the mansion, including a wine cellar.

While two and one-half acres of grounds surround the house, it is far short of the beautiful ten acres where once flourished formal gardens and spreading lawns, all kept to perfection.

After spending many years of gracious living in the mansion, the Watkins' sold it to a wealthy bachelor planter, Samuel H. Moore. It was he who ordered the marble mantels from Italy and the bronze chandeliers from France to add refined touches of beauty to the place.

The new owner entertained on a scale abundantly lavish. It was here that he gave the most famous ball ever held in Alabama. It honored a cow, not just another cow, but "Lily Flag," his prize Jersey which had just been judged at the 1893 Chicago World's Fair, as the world's champion butter producer. The ball cost thousands of dollars. Special dance floors were built. An orchestra was brought down from Nashville. Rare wine and champagne was imported from Spain and France. Fifty kinds of cake were served to hundreds of guests who came in response to the special engraved invitations—they came from such distant places as New York, California and Illinois. And "Lily Flag," bedecked with a garland of red roses about her neck, was stationed at the head of the reception line where she mooed greetings to the guests as they arrived.

After his death, the home passed to Kate Barnard, Mr. Moore's niece, and a few years later, to Mrs. Margaret DuBose Smith. It was the latter who added the four Corinthian columns to the front portico. Then for some twenty years it was the property of the David A. Graysons, a family which had long been prominent in southern colonial history. One of the Grayson ancestors, Colonel William Grayson, was aide-de-camp to General George Washington during the Revolutionary War, as well as one of the first two senators elected from the State of Virginia.

In recent years ownership passed to the Milton K. Cummins', who have been exceedingly generous in their love and maintenance of the place, keeping it always in a splendid state of preservation and beauty. And, too, they have perpetuated a hospitable way of life which has nearly always been found at this oasis of good living.

Watkins House. Front view.

Watkins House. An ancestral portrait is the focal point of the dining room furnished with an Empire set with claw-footed legs.

Watkins House. The spiral staircase in the entrance hall is one of three such stairs in the house built by James Bell, a negro slave carpenter, who devoted three years to the task.

Watkins House. The superbly carved Carrara marble mantel is greatly enriched by the hand-carved rosewood trimming of these two John Belter sofas covered in apple green satin. The twin parlors are furnished in identical manner.

58

THE BIBB MANSION, Huntsville, Alabama

Oh, where is there today the father who builds for his daughter the equivalent of a $32,000.00 ante-bellum mansion!

But Thomas Bibb was no ordinary man. He was an aristocratic planter, holding ownership to thousands of acres of fertile crop lands, and he had just served as second governor of the State of Alabama. He built this stately mansion at 303 Williams Street in Huntsville for his daughter, Adeline, who had married James Bradley. Several written dates have been given for the building of the house, but one item seems significant: it had its gala opening in the form of a housewarming given in honor of the Bradley's daughter, Susan, when she was married to Thomas White, the year being 1832.

That housewarming was a function long remembered in Huntsville society. The long table which held the stacks of china plates, cut glass dessert dishes, bowls and heirloom decorative pieces—all beautiful and valuable to the Bibb's and Bradley's—broke from the weight, and the floor beneath was piled with a heaping debris of shattered glass and broken china. And the housewarming turned out to be a goosepimply affair.

There are probably more errors and myths about this house than about any other prominent home in the state. It is most often recorded as being the William Wyatt Bibb home, he being a brother of Thomas. However, Thomas did not even own the land where the house now stands when his brother died in 1820. He bought it a year later from John Reed, and the house was not started until the late 1820's.

It is kindly of people to want to credit this pillar of Ionic architecture to William Wyatt Bibb, for its tremendous Greek temple façade is big, bold, massive and masculine, and until this day wears a mien of sturdiness and endurance suggestive of an Egyptian Pharaoh's pyramidal tomb. William Wyatt Bibb was like that: big, bold, classical, and a character of long enduring.

A legislator from the State of Georgia; a congressman and a United States senator also from Georgia; a doctor of medicine from the University of Pennsylvania; territorial governor of Alabama, and lastly, first governor of the State of Alabama—such were the accomplishments of the forty short years of his life. This man of much and varied learning, compassion and wisdom was one of Alabama's truly great men.

It is true that he resided temporarily in Huntsville during the first legislative session held by the new state after it was formed there in 1819, but the Bibb House was not even built at that time. William Wyatt Bibb's plantation home was in Autauga (now Elmore) County at Coosada. It was there that Bibb was thrown from a mule during a thunderstorm and died shortly afterwards, July 10, 1820. He is buried in the family burial ground there on the old plantation, but his house no longer stands, it having burned in the late 1890's.

Thomas Bibb had already built a priceless mansion for himself at Belle Mina. It was finished in 1826, and it was about that time that he decided to build the Bibb House for his daughter in Huntsville. Glancing through the story of his life, one has the feeling that he desired to build this mansion as something of an artistic hobby, to perfect in it any points which might have seemed to him flaws in Belle Mina. For instance, he added a grandiose pediment to the portico, whereas Belle Mina had a simple hipped roof. And here he chose spectacular stone columns with elaborate Ionic capitals to support the pediment, making for one of the loveliest and most architectually perfect Greek Revival porticoes to be found anywhere. It appears from all points of view to be the sturdiest grand manner mansion in Alabama.

Whether Bibb actually designed and built the house himself is not known; however, it seems likely that he did, for records show that he was awarded part of the construction work on the Madison County courthouse shortly after this house was finished. Thus he was a builder.

Meticulous journals were kept on the mansion which show that $32,000.00 was spent on its construction, a tidy sum when it is considered that slaves did the brick making on the scene.

As beautiful as the pillars and pediment are, it is the bricks themselves which are possessed with the most exciting character. They have a purplish sienna tone, almost like the soft lavender hues of late sunset falling across newly plowed earth. They were soaked under water to give lasting wear and durability, and until this day they do not show the faintest sign of deterioration. Herein again is an example where the ingenuity of the pioneer builder fitted his materials to his needs, and emerged with an accomplishment of architectural refinement.

Inside, the mansion is finished with deft and exceedingly good workmanship. The carved mantels are of particularly good design. Three-panel folding doors open from the sumptuous entrance hall to the library on one side and the drawing room on the other. At the far end of the hall is the staircase with its double landing. The brick partitions between the rooms are three-feet in thickness.

Thomas Bibb died, September 30, 1839, and the house was not to remain long in the Bibb family. Thomas Bradley, who suffered financial set-backs in the cotton business in New Orleans, had to sell the house in 1844 to meet his obligations. It was bought by Andrew Beirne, whose son, George P. Beirne and his descendants, lived there for more than seventy years. From the Beirnes it went to a nephew, Howard Thomas, who sold it in 1920 to W. E. Butler. Then in 1927 it was purchased by the W. W. Newmans and again fell into the proud Bibb hands, Mrs. Newman being a great-great-granddaughter of Thomas Bibb.

The house was used as a Union headquarters during the Civil War, and Gen. William Tecumseh Sherman stopped there on one occasion. Visitors used to be shown the slick worn brick on the front walk where the guards walked to and fro at their sentinel post, keeping watch over the headquarters.

The home is surrounded with a profusion of boxwood as old as the house itself, along with beautiful foliage of spruce, pine, oak and magnolia.

Bibb Mansion. Ionic columns at their very best were used to beautify the superb portico.

Bibb Mansion. Only the very sturdiest of materials and the finest of workmanship were employed in its construction, completed in 1832.

OAK LAWN, Huntsville, Alabama

Though one of the finest of Alabama's ante-bellum mansions, Oak Lawn all too frequently has been overlooked when mention has been made of the state's early homes. This may well be due to the fact that no renowned statesman has lived there, and no president has been entertained at Oak Lawn. However the fact remains that few early mansions can boast of such sturdy workmanship, geared always to a pattern of stability, yet pleasing in architectural execution.

The plantation upon which Oak Lawn is built is located two miles west of Huntsville on the Fayetteville pike. It nestles in a broad valley of red clay, famed for its prolific cotton.

Settlers came early to the region. Indians were still solidly entrenched. It was on October 4, 1809 that John W. Walker arrived in Twickenham, later called Huntsville, and on that date bought his plantation land from the United States government. It remained, however, for someone else to build Oak Lawn upon the land which he purchased that day. How soon afterwards the mansion was started remains a matter of conjecture. The dates are not even revealed in the abstract to the property. However, historians give John Robinson credit for the completed job, even though incomplete records point to the possibility that any one of the three, John F. Newman, William Fleming or Lemuel Mead may have had a hand in its building, since all of them owned the plantation prior to its passing to Robinson in 1844.

It seems most likely that to Robinson must go the credit for Oak Lawn as it stands today. This is supported by the fact that Oak Lawn was almost a twin to Forest Field, before it burned, another stately mansion built nearby by Charles Robinson, a brother to John.

Oak Lawn suggests a strong influence of tidewater colonial architecture, in the massing of side wings projecting beyond the main body of the house. Very few examples of this style are to be found in ante-bellum Alabama. The two wings serve as large bedrooms, and each has a shutter-covered door opening onto the spacious veranda.

There is a beautiful simplicity in the fenestration of the veranda. The windows are unusually well spaced, and neither they nor the doors are burdened by ornate heads. The entire length of the veranda wall is without ornamentation but for two slightly protruding pilasters at either end, each bearing the mere suggestion of a capital. The commodious front entrance lends a touch of finesse in the delicately conceived transom and sidelights with their many tiny window sections. The four columns are of plain Doric, set on limestone bases. And the handmade brick which floor the veranda also line the walkway leading out to the circular drive where stands the original horse block. The walk is bordered with handsome boxwood.

The two great halls, which extend the full length of both floors, are fifty feet long and fourteen feet in width and height. They are connected by a U-shaped staircase, guarded by a cherrywood banister. A plain wooden frieze caps the decorative touch of the halls. The door casings in the halls are simple and somewhat crude, compared with those in the parlors. The hall lamps hang from twin bronze medallions of clustered roses and curled leaves.

Twin parlors, with folding doors that all but make for a single enormous room, extend the full depth of the house. It is here that Oak Lawn assumes its greatest charm, for the rooms were conceived in an air of exceptional refinement and flooded with sunlight from an abundance of spacious windows. A tall pier mirror, fitted in parallelism at the far end of either parlor, affords reflections and counter-reflections of the two bronze chandeliers, frilled with tiny sword-clad warriors and smiling cherubs. The mirrors overhanging the twin marble mantels are bordered by plain rolled gold frames, as are the pier mirrors. Only the front parlor has a frieze, although there are indications which suggest that the other parlor walls were once so trimmed.

Every bedroom in the house is a corner room, planned as such for comfortable ventilation during summer heat.

During the Civil War, Oak Lawn was used by the Union Army as an officers' quarters, while the troops camped upon the spreading lawn. Then during the Spanish-American War, troops again returned to Oak Lawn and bivouacked there for many months, the mansion being used as a hospital. Many temporary partitions were erected in the halls and rooms to make wards.

In 1919 the home was purchased by W. P. Dilworth, after having been unoccupied for many years. Neglect had left its mark of deterioration upon the once splendid dwelling, and it remained for the Dilworth's to bring about a complete restoration. From haylofts and chicken nests, they restored the place to the state of beauty which it had known in earlier years. Their restoration was so noteworthy that *Country Home* magazine featured it in a pictorial lay-out.

In the early 1940's Oak Lawn came into possession of the Max Luthers, devotees of fine show horses. Specializing in five-gaited horses, Mr. Luther has taken dozens of prizes at horse shows all over the country. His horse, "Sally Co-Ed," was judged world's champion in the fine harness class at the Madison Square Garden show in November, 1948. Her owner refused an offer of $30,000.00 for the noble champion, which only six months later died from a spider bite.

And so at Oak Lawn, where once plodded cotton plowing mules, today prance beautiful champion show horses which have won so many trophies and ribbons that a special glass case had to be built in the upstairs hall to accommodate them.

Oak Lawn is Alabama's finest example of a mansion with wings added to either side, an influence derived from the Colonial Period in Virginia and other eastern seaboard colonies.

WINSTON PLACE, Valley Head, Alabama

The sprawling veranda is the crowning motif of beautiful Winston Place, nestled at the foot of Lookout Mountain in the century old town of Valley Head. This impressive lavishness of the veranda, both upstairs and down, is undoubtedly one of the state's finest examples of how the master builders planned for the luxurious and open air living which the slave supported plantations made possible in ante-bellum days.

Winston Place had its origin in a dog-trot log house. Actually, one downstairs bedroom still has the ceiling timbers which once were a part of that simple pioneer construction. But when the Honorable William Overton Winston first bought the 3,000 surrounding acres in 1835, he envisioned more than the mere dogtrot; he foresaw the magnificent mansion which was to rise from the crude log house, and future years brought with them the complete fulfillment of his dreams.

A few Red Men still lingered at Valley Head when William Overton Winston and a colony of Virginia and Carolina settlers planted their roots so deep into the valley soil that they have never strayed, even until this day.

A giant red oak tree in the corner of Winston Place yard served for many years as a Council Tree for the Cherokees. And one of the Indians is buried on the lawn, only a few yards from the old Council Tree.

A few of the Cherokees stayed behind, when their tribe began moving westward in the early 1830's, and helped the 40-odd Winston slaves in the building of Winston Place. Bricks for the eight fireplaces and glass panes for the ninety-four windows were made on the grounds, while many of the great timber sills were carted by oxen for more than thirty miles across Sand Mountain.

Mr. Winston, a man of learning and wisdom, claimed as his cousin, the distinguished Dolly Madison and Patrick Henry. While back in England, Sarah Winston, from the same family, became the direct progenitor of the great Winston Churchill of today.

But the proud builder of Winston Place achieved success in his own right. He began the practice of law when the DeKalb region became a county in 1836. He served fifteen years in the state legislature, and was elected to the Secession Convention of 1861, and to the Constitutional Convention of 1865. But perhaps his most lasting contribution to the state was the promotion of Wills Valley Railroad, of which he served as the first president. This road extended from Chattanooga southward into Alabama, and later became part of the Alabama Great Southern, one of the South's greatest railroads of today.

He died in 1871—age 67—and was buried in the family cemetery on the plantation place. Today a magnificent magnolia shades his grave from the bright sun of summer and protects it from the snows of winter.

He left behind a monument in the magnificence of Winston Place, where, down through the years, many notables, including kinsman Governor John A. Winston of Alabama, Lady Irene Whittaker of London, England, and Governor James E. Folsom, have been entertained.

For one hundred and nine years the mansion remained in the Winston family. In later years it came to be known as the Anderson Place, and then the Tutwiler Mansion, the names being taken from Winston daughters and granddaughters who married into these families and made their home at Winston Place. It was not until 1944, when the place was sold to Haralson Hammond and family that the grand mansion passed from the Winston family.

Winston Place has seen a multiplicity of varied existence. The first mistress of the new home, Maria Louise Winston, being a woman of unusual religious devotion, organized the first Presbyterian church of Valley Head in her parlor. She took upon herself the task of holding regular services, and old folks around Valley Head still refer to the eloquent sermons she delivered. She also worked devotedly at instructing the slaves in the teachings of the Scripture.

Then at one time during the Civil War, Winston Place teemed with Yankee Blue Coats. In the Fall of 1863, 30,000 Union troops camped on the Winston plantation. Their commander, Gen. Jefferson Davis of Lexington, Kentucky—reputedly no kin to the Confederate president—made his headquarters at the mansion.

During this visit of the Blue Coats, one of the Winston slaves gathered up the family silver and hid it in the twenty-five-foot dry well in the backyard where it remained in safety during the seizure, the soldiers thinking it was an ordinary well and not one for cold storage purposes only. After leaving Valley Head, the Union troops moved northward and engaged in the battle of Chickamauga.

A sprawling lilac bush in the yard is a headstone as well as a producer of beautiful flowers. Once when a family of pioneers were heading west by wagon, they stopped at Winston Place to get help for their sick baby. But it was too late. The baby died and was buried beside the flower garden. And at the request of its mother, a lilac bush was planted upon the grave so that new blossoms of life could burst forth each spring and scatter purple petals over the infant's resting site.

In later years when Major F. Y. Anderson, who had married a granddaughter of William Overton Winston, became the master of Winston Place, he entertained with such lavishness that a six-room wing was added, making the house U-shaped. But in the early 1930's the Tutwilers removed the wing and restored the mansion to its original floor plan.

The present veranda with its great Doric columns was not a part of the mansion as it was first conceived. This entire portico was added at an undetermined later date.

One of the unusual sights to be found on the grounds today is the octagonal house, used for curing meat. A small domical opening at the top permits the hickory curing smoke to escape. This is one of the few such auxiliary buildings remaining in Alabama today which was built in the classical pattern of the 'Big House.'

Winston Place has the queen veranda of all the ante-bellum mansions in the state. Even with all the sumptuousness of its spreading dimensions, there is applied architectural restraint which gives it orderliness, gracefulness, and enduring charm.

This side view of the veranda pinpoints the extraordinary beauty of the Doric columns.

CHAPTER III

Talladega—Birmingham—Tuscaloosa Region

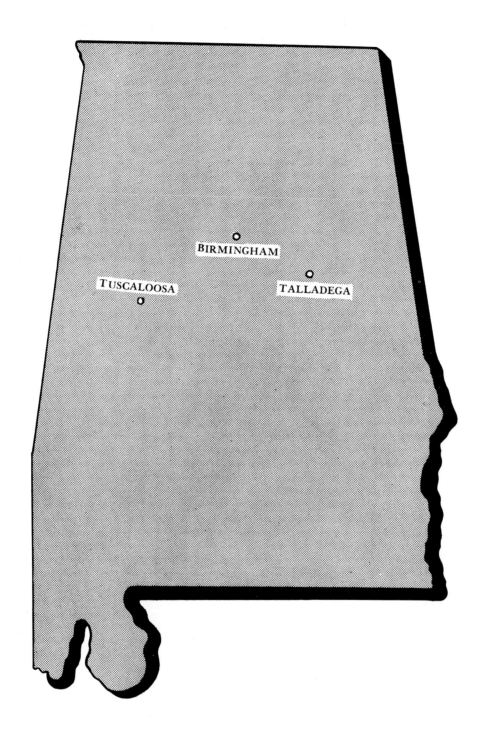

(Talladega—Birmingham—Tuscaloosa Region)

PLOWMAN HOME, Talladega, Alabama

In Talladega, a city which very early applied good architecture to its mansions, Captain Albert Plowman added resplendent taste to the flourishing Greek Revival when he built his town house around 1850.

The delightful Doric portico, with a thrust of masculinity in the broad entablature and a risqué bit of finery in the handsomely balustraded balcony, is but the crowning touch of a house which is masterfully built throughout.

Captain Plowman married Idora McClellan, daughter of General William B. McClellan whose plantation and brick mansion, Idlewild, is located about three miles from Talledega. This must have been a happy union, because three of the Plowman boys married three McClellan sisters.

The Plowman Home became widely known, in that for many years it was the home of Idora McClellan Plowman, who, under the pen name of Betsy Hamilton, became a nationally published writer of Negro and plantation life stories. A memorial library is established in her honor at Alabama College, Montevallo.

Set in a beautifully terraced grove of trees and century-old boxwood, the home in recent years was purchased by Julian Elliott.

Talladega's most beautiful Doric colonnaded mansion, is remembered as the home of Betsy Hamilton, writer of noteworthy significance.

MOUNT IDA, near Talladega, Alabama

Almost beneath the shadow of a rolling blue mountain known as Sleeping Giant, Walker Reynolds in 1833 purchased his first tract of Talladega County land from the Oche-hadjo, one of the Creek Indian tribes. The deed to the land bore the personal signatures of several Creek Indians, and the bill of sale was later approved in Washington by President John Tyler, "in the sixty-eighth year of the Independence of the United States."

For some time the Indians lived within sight of the Reynolds home, and even though there prevailed a peaceful relationship, occasionally embitterments flared up. During the course of time, Reynolds repeatedly missed cattle from his herd. It was after such an incident that he took his shotgun in hand and went in search of a missing yearling. While riding deep into the woods, he came upon a Creek in the act of skinning the young calf. When the Indian saw him, he dashed for his gun propped against a nearby tree, but Reynolds was quicker, and fired a wad of buckshot into the Redskin's leg. But the shot failed to down the Creek and he leveled his gun at Reynolds, who had dashed behind a tree to recharge his muzzle loader. The Indian's volley ripped the bark from the tree and a bullet burned the hide from the white man's stomach. Reynolds then pounced upon the Indian, took him prisoner, and escorted him to the jail in Talladega where he was charged with cattle rustling. This incident throws a light on Reynolds' character, in that it would have been far simpler to have killed the Indian instead of turning him over to the law for proper justice to be administered. It was by such actions that he was able thereafter to live peacefully among the Red Men, and at the same time, command their respect.

And, too, squire Reynolds was good to his slaves. By 1864 there were, according to the records, as many as two hundred, an exceedingly large number for even a wealthy planter. The majority of the slaves stayed on as freed men after the Emancipation Proclamation, and the master allotted each family a farming acreage, a house, and a mule.

The greatest feast ever held at Mount Ida was in honor of two slaves—Uncle Ben, the driver or head man of all the slaves, and his wife, Aunt Jennie, head of the house servants. Aunt Jennie had supervised the rearing of all the Reynolds children and was lovingly called, Mammy, while Uncle Ben was known as Daddy. The celebration was in honor of their golden anniversary. The dining table was extended to its fullest length and piled high with a vast array of anniversary gifts. Every child who had grown up under their watchful eyes, as well as every grandchild, bore gifts. And while all the Negroes, freed men now, lined one side of the banquet hall, members of the Reynolds family paid glowing verbal tributes to the faith, devotion, and loving-kindness of Uncle Ben and Aunt Jennie. The celebration ended by the two honored guests pledging anew their lasting love by the token of a bridal kiss.

Another great occasion at Mount Ida took place in 1886 when Maud, the youngest daughter, was married. Her wedding gown was the finest that money could buy, and in 1939, when the world premiere of "Gone With The Wind" was held in Atlanta, this same dress took second place in a South-wide contest to select the finest wedding gowns of ante-bellum days.

Today when a stranger inquires about Mount Ida, he is apt to hear that it is the place where they have a gold mine in the front yard and a dungeon under the house. But upon closer scrutiny, one finds that the gold mine was once an ore pit, and the dungeon, twenty-eight feet deep and twelve feet wide at the bottom, was once a cistern. And however adventurous the tale might sound about when the master used to throw unruly slaves into the pit, it is all without a vestige of truth.

The most imposing feature of Mount Ida is the magnificent veranda, edged by six superbly fluted columns topped by inverted bell-shaped capitals, a motif extremely rare among ante-bellum homes in the state. Another rare feature of the columns is the foot-rest, a semi-circular iron bar attached to each shaft of the colonnade. These foot-rests permitted greatly added comfort, allowing those who sat looking out over the vast expanse of farmland to rear back and prop up their feet in luxurious comfort. These are the only such foot-props known to exist in the entire realm of Alabama's ante-bellum mansions. The columns are of brick and plaster, and for lasting durability, marble squares were used not only for the column bases, but also for the front steps. This marble came from one of the quarries in Talladega, only a few miles away. An over-hanging balcony, extending the full length of the veranda, is guarded by unusually fine ironlace fashioned after the lyre. Simply by raising the sashes and opening the wooden aprons at the bottom, the four tall windows are transformed into doors, allowing passageways from the two front parlors onto the veranda. These are in addition to the well carpentered central entrances, both upstairs and down. The sidelights and transoms have beautiful amethyst glass. Sections of the sidelights feature a fruit-laden grapevine, climbing from bottom to top, while the transom panes have crystal-cut clusters of roses standing out like sparkling diamonds as one peers out from the interior hall.

Since the house was built in three sections, the original roof was pitched in three parallel gables of saw-tooth arrangement. To dispose of the rainwater, metal scuppers were built at each end of the roof troughs, and as the water came rushing down, the scuppers shot it out and away from the side of the house. This was a precaution against deterioration since there were no drains on the house. A false roof has since been erected over the gables, but the scuppers remain.

The fourteen rooms of the interior are finished in fine and well preserved timbers, especially the two-inch thick heart pine flooring, planed only on the top side. The house plan is centered around the great hall, with spacious rooms on either side. The straight stairway of the hall is unique in that, instead of starting its rise from the front of the hall, it commences at the back. This was made necessary because the master wanted it to open into the front section of the upstairs which was the girls' suite of rooms. A solid wall originally extended across the entire center of the upstairs, cutting off the back rooms as an apartment, or *garçonnière,* for the boys, who entered from a separate stairway in the rear of the house. To relieve the abruptness of the staircase in reverse, the master built a niche beneath it, and for many decades it held a Rip Van Winkle piece of sculpture. The central hall was once papered with a rich black and gold paper featuring the Seven Muses.

Beyond a doubt, Mount Ida has the most highly decorated false grain wainscoting to be found in Alabama. All of the upstairs rooms, including the doors, were finished in this elaborate false paneling by an artist brought from New York. The mantels throughout the house are simple and unpretentious. All but two are of marblized wood.

In 1859, the year the house was finally completed, Walker and Hannah Reynolds journeyed to New York where they purchased the furniture. By now, Reynolds had become a man of unlimited weath and it was his desire that the mansion be replete with the finest that could be had. The front parlor was the most elaborate room. Called 'The Blue Room,' it was finished as a replica of the chamber in The White House which bore the same name. Heavy gilded cornices topped the tall windows, decorated with rich blue drapes, gilt trimmed. The two sofas and the many chairs were upholstered in exquisite blue silk, with all the carved trim done in gilt. A one-piece Axminister rug of matching blue gave to the room a quality of distinction and color tone seldom seen in the frontiers of Alabama.

The days of enjoying the hospitality of Mount Ida were brief, for hardly had the master and his family settled in the completed mansion when the drums of war began to roll. Rousseau's Raiders invaded Talladega and rode on to Mount Ida where they raided the smokehouse and pantries, as well as taking the slaves and thirty-two mules and horses. The crop of wheat and the gin warehouse containing two hundred bales of cotton were burned by an unknown culprit. And so, Mount Ida was left a great expanse of emptiness—gone were the Negroes who worked the fields, and gone were the mules that pulled the plows. But widow Hannah Reynolds managed the plantation until her death in 1890, at which time it was divided among the descendants.

Reynolds died in 1871 at the age of seventy-two. His greatest achievements were by no means limited to planting. In 1849 he was elected to the legislature by the Whig Party and he made an enviable record of service. He was an ardent Whig supporter until 1860, at which time he threw his entire fortune behind the Confederate struggle. He was the guiding mind in the construction of the Alabama and Tennessee Rivers Railway, extending from Selma to Rome to Dalton. As a stockholder, he backed the venture by purchasing $100,000.00 in bonds, and during the building days he helped overcome the financial anxiety of many worried stockholders. When the road was dedicated, July 15, 1858, the people of Talladega presented him a silver pitcher, extolling his "energetic, liberal, and enterprising" efforts.

Mount Ida remained in the Reynolds family until 1922, at which time it was sold and all the original furnishings divided among the descendants.

The fine old mansion has since passed through several ownerships, and it fared none the better for having done so, until Mr. and Mrs. R. B. Kent purchased it in 1949. Mr. Kent, one of Alabama's leading Jersey cattlemen, has transformed the long neglected and run-down plantation into broad fields of clover and rye and winter grasses where his prize herd grazes the year round.

The house itself has fared equally as well. Mrs. Kent has done one of the finest restoration jobs to be found in any of the state's ante-bellum mansions. Working with the aid and suggestion of some Reynolds descendants, she has tried meticulously to restore the house to its original grandeur. Furnishings in keeping with the period were painstakingly selected. The results are such that one not knowing the story, would

74

never know that every piece of furniture had not been there from the very beginning. The mansion throughout has an air of classical refinement, charm, and gracious living.

There is something consoling and proper in the fact that the builder of Mount Ida is buried in the family cemetery only a stone's throw from the mansion. Upon his headstone is carved the following epitaph, didactic enough to make any passer-by pause in contemplation:

"Whether curiosity or affaction shall lead you to this spot, and whether friends or strangers shall trace these lines—yet let this solemn impression rest on the mind and deeply impress the heart: This is the work of death! This is the end which awaits all the living, and you, too, must die!"

Mount Ida. The reverse stairway makes for an interesting hall. Note the clustered grape design in the amethyst glass transom and sidelights.

Mount Ida. Century old magnolias and a lush growth of boxwood all but hide the approach.

Mount Ida. The guest parlor, originally known as "The Blue Room," is lavish with Victorian decorations. The pier mirrors and window cornices are especially fine. The mantel is of marbelized wood.

Mount Ida. The dining room chairs are Early American and blend well with the high, bold mantel. The pastoral wall paper has the effect of bringing the farm right into the room.

Mount Ida. Superbly fluted columns with bell-shaped capitals put Mount Ida in a class all by itself, for no other such exquisite columns are to be found in Alabama.

ALPINE, near Talladega, Alabama

Alpine is located about ten miles west of Talladega in a broad valley of fertile plantation land. The plantation in time developed into a small community, also named Alpine, with its depot, Baptist church, and tiny cluster of rural stores and dwellings.

When Oliver Welch arrived there with his family from Virginia in 1834 and bought up the land, it was thickly wooded of virgin timber. With the help of a few family slaves, he quickly built an unpretentious, two-story log house known as Kingston.

It remained for his son, Nathaniel Welch, to build Alpine, two miles over from Kingston. Situated on the crest of a long rolling knoll, Alpine has a most breath-taking approach lined with ancient oaks, and extending almost a quarter of a mile down to the railroad.

An expert carpenter named A. D. Bell built Alpine during the spring, summer and fall of 1858. And while Alpine is not one of the finest homes in Alabama, it is certainly one of the most interesting plantation type houses. For instance, where else can one find this beautiful window arrangement of the façade? The builder carried the idea of sidelights to the windows, with the result that the four windows at the front have the main window supplemented on either side by sidelights of one pane width. This fenestration is indeed clever and shows that the carpenter desired to utilize something other than the routine pattern for windows.

The façade of Alpine, in its simplicity, is a lovely thing. The four Doric pillars are of excellent design, topped with the proper abacus which is all too often subdued in size. The recessed entrance with sidelights and rectangular transom is identical both upstairs and down. The whipsawn weatherboarding beneath the portico is applied without over-lapping and makes for a smooth finish. The fluted pilasters are unusually broad. But the finest thing about Alpine is the exquisite finery of the ornamental iron balcony, certainly a most delicate and beautiful grille pattern.

Note should be made also of Alpine's foundation. It is made of sawn blocks of tough, yellowish-brown stone taken from Talladega County quarries. The foundation rises to four feet at the front and provides for a very unique interior arrangement. Under the left side of the house is built a long room, twenty by forty feet. This room is used as the dining room. A stone stairway, with swags worn into the steps, rises to the first floor. In later years the rear of this room was set off by a partition and a modern kitchen installed. This cellar dining room plan certainly exemplifies the spirit of the plantation owner's individuality, and pinpoints his idea of practicality, for such a plan makes for cool dining even in the hottest days of summer, to say nothing of added warmth during the winter months. The room is lighted with half-windows set into the foundation stone. Perhaps no other single spot in Alabama would so quickly transplant one into the ante-bellum atmosphere of plantation life as a visit to the cellar dining hall of Alpine.

The house is not square as one would gather from looking at the front. It is L-shaped, with the L extending to the left rear. The staircase is quite simple, as are the mantels throughout the house except for the ones in the parlor and guest bedroom and they are marbelized wood, a decorative device used in several of the Talladega mansions, but found very little in other parts of the state.

Alpine until this day has remained in the Welch family, a very happy fact indeed. And the fine manner in which it has been preserved bespeaks the Welch's love for their ancestral home.

Alpine. The cellar dining hall is unique, and the ornamental iron balcony is the finest in the state.

MUDD-MUNGER HOME, Birmingham, Alabama

Many express surprise that an ante-bellum mansion exists in Birmingham, a city which was not founded until July, 1871. There are several such mansions, the finest of which is the Mudd-Munger Home, it having been built in a broad fertile valley some forty years before the founding of the city.

Shortly after his marriage to Florence Earle, December 22, 1841, William S. Mudd purchased a hundred-acre tract from his father-in-law and set about building a pretentious mansion. Mudd was one of the founders of the Elyton Land Company which promoted real estate development in the community of Elyton, which later became part of Birmingham.

The mansion is located only about fifteen blocks from downtown Birmingham, straight west on First Avenue, North. The grounds, although greatly reduced from the original acreage, are spacious and beautiful, covering the better part of two city blocks. The giant trees are still there, and in the springtime buttercups pop up yellow across the rolling and sloping lawn.

The property was sold to Henry Fairchild DeBardeleben, Birmingham mining magnate, in 1884, and he soon afterwards sold it to F. H. Whitney of Iowa. Then in 1902 it was purchased by Robert S. Munger, developer of the "Munger system" of controlling cotton lint in gins, and it has remained in his family ever since. It is owned today by Mr. and Mrs. Alex C. Montgomery, Mrs. Montgomery being the former Ruby Munger, daughter of Robert S. Munger.

The Mudd-Munger place is one of the few fine mansions using the square pillars such as found at Bluff Hall in Demopolis and the Robert Loveman home in Tuscaloosa. It is also one of the few which has a complete upstairs veranda.

The mansion has a commodious central hall with straight-run stairway, and a parlor extending the full length of the house. It has been exceedingly well maintained down through the years.

Mudd-Munger home takes its name from two of Birmingham's most industrially prominent families. Its square pillared portico overlooks two city blocks of beautiful grounds.

82

THE PRESIDENT'S MANSION—UNIVERSITY OF ALABAMA,
Tuscaloosa, Alabama

It has long been customary for the universities of the nation to have a place of residence set aside for the president of the institution. The University of Alabama was no exception. The University was founded in 1831 and nine years later its president, Dr. Basil Manly, moved into the new and imposing edifice. Since 1840, sixteen presidents have lived there.

When members of the state legislature voted funds for the new President's Mansion, they expressed the desire for a house of much beauty, one in keeping with the great emphasis put upon classical learning at the time. It was therefore agreed to hire an accomplished architect to execute the plans, a move which was rather revolutionary for Alabama at the time, since very few architects had ever done work in the state.

The man chosen was William Nichols, an Englishman who had offices in Philadelphia. However, he was not a stranger to Alabama. He had designed the state capitol in Tuscaloosa when the capital was moved there in 1826—a building rather disappointing when compared with some of his later works, since it looked more like a courthouse than a capitol building. This structure was destroyed by fire in 1923.

When the old Mississippi state capitol was about half built, defective workmanship was found and Nichols was commissioned in 1835 to finish the job. It was for this building that Nichols received national acclaim, and architects still point to the old building, restored in 1916 with the senate and house chambers replaced with rooms, as one of the most creative architectural works in all the South. Nichols also designed the Mississippi governor's mansion in 1842, immediately following his work on the University dwelling.

One has but to look at the President's Mansion to see that Nichols had free rein to build as lavish an edifice as his heart desired. Naturally, he chose the Greek Revival because it was the style which dominated all sumptuous buildings during this period, and Nichols himself was one of its foremost exponents.

In the President's Mansion, Nichols started with a ground floor, upon which he added the two main stories of the house. For the two top floors, he built a majestic Neo-Classical façade, in which the Ionic order was employed in the six lofty columns. Heavy boxlike dentiling set off a beautifully proportioned entablature. Then across the full length of the veranda, as well as across the exceedingly long third floor balcony, Nichols added iron grillework. He also had a similar grille pattern across the front of the porch roof, but this was later removed. Then, he added the final touch of beauty in the superb doorway with its delicate Greek trim.

At this point, Nichols broke from the confines of the Greek Revival. He built a double winding stone staircase from the ground to the first floor and trimmed it too with grillework. Arches, which the Greeks never used, topped the five entrances of the ground floor loggia. Thus we find here a most beautiful and richly conceived Greek Revival portico. It is all the more pleasing, due to the originality of the ground floor innovation. This design set a style for many other later buildings on the University campus.

Only the front of the house was stuccoed and painted white according to Nichols' plans. The sides remained in natural brick finish until years later, when the entire exterior was finished like the façade.

All three floors are divided by a central hall, and on either side of each hall are two rooms. The floor plans today are somewhat modified from the original ones, but care has been taken not to change the general character which Nichols put into the house. On the ground floor the two front chambers were bedrooms and the one to the right rear served as the kitchen. A staircase extended from the kitchen entrance to the original dining room directly above. However, this is no longer the arrangement. A modern kitchen has been built on the first floor and the dining room has replaced the parlor at the left front. The top floor consists of four bedrooms.

It is on the first floor where the rooms of showiness are to be found. Excellent medallions of plaster center the double parlors on the right. The cornice trim of the rooms also is very good. But the rooms are somewhat marred in beauty by the ornate wooden mantels which undoubtedly were added during the Victorian splurge. One cannot conceivably imagine Nichols allowing such mediocre mantels to go into his otherwise classical mansion. A spiral staircase sets off the broad depth of the entrance hall. The hall chandelier, as well as the one in the dining room—both of which were added recently, are exceedingly handsome.

The mansion is one of four structures left standing when Federal troops under the command of General John T. Croxton set fire to the University buildings, April 4, 1865. The sparing of the house is credited to the daring wife of President Landon C. Garland who dashed in and ordered Croxton's Raiders to extinguish the fire which had already been kindled in the hall, and they obligingly obeyed her command.

After the war it was planned to use the ground floor of the President's Mansion for the reopening of the University, but only one student presented himself, and classes were not begun until 1870 when buildings had been constructed.

All in all, the President's Mansion is probably the state's most imposing Greek Revival mansion. Its entire conception embodies much originality. It has line and form and character all its own, and nowhere in the state is there a mansion which even resembles it slightly. Its enduring magnificence is a lasting tribute to the ingeniousness of its architect, William Nichols.

The President's Mansion at the University has the raised cottage motif adapted to the grand manner mansion.

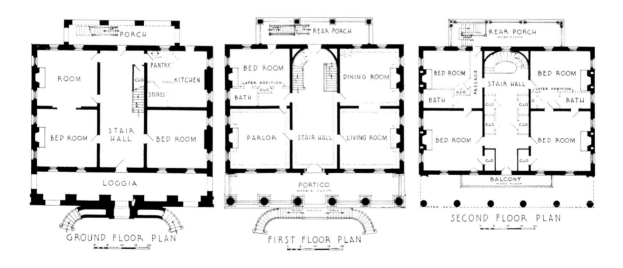

GROUND FLOOR PLAN

FIRST FLOOR PLAN

SECOND FLOOR PLAN

The President's Mansion. The spiral staircase in the central hall is excellently proportioned. Stairway at right descends to ground floor rooms.

The hallway chandelier, hanging from the acanthus scrolled medallion, is reflected in buffet mirror.

The plaster medallion in each of the twin parlors is exceptionally delicate.

86

THE GORGAS HOME, Tuscaloosa, Alabama

William Crawford Gorgas is Alabama's greatest man, and the Gorgas Home in Tuscaloosa has been made a state shrine by the Alabama legislature in tribute to his greatness.

Historians repeatedly refer to William Crawford Gorgas as "the world's greatest sanitarian." This man of health giving service came from great stock. His father, General Josiah Gorgas, was Confederate Chief of Ordnance and seventh president of the University of Alabama, serving from 1878-79. His mother, Amelia Gayle Gorgas, is one of Alabama's most beloved women. She was the daughter of Governor and Mrs. John Gayle and lived in Tuscaloosa while her father served as governor at the state capital there. Later she spent her young days in Washington where her father was United States Congressman. She was a frequent visitor at the White House, a protege of John C. Calhoun, and one of the two women seated on the platform during the laying of the Washington Monument cornerstone. Her greatest contribution to Alabama, though, was during the period from 1883 to 1906 when she served as librarian of the University of Alabama. The University's fine new library is named in her honor, the Amelia Gayle Gorgas Library.

However, none were to attain greatness in the manner of the renowned William Crawford Gorgas who was born in Mobile, October 3, 1854, and died in London, England, July 4, 1920. Gorgas became famous for applying Major Walter Reed's discovery of the prevention of yellow fever to actual use. He rose to international prominence, first when he ridded Havana of the dreaded fever, and then again in 1904 when he cleared the scourge from Panama and opened the way for completion of the ambitious Atlantic-Pacific waterway, the Panama Canal. He was made a colonel in the United States Army by a special act of Congress. Later, he became surgeon general of the United States Army, first with the rank of brigadier general, then major general. Then in 1918 he joined the Rockefeller Foundation as director of yellow fever research work, and director of the International Health Board. He did extensive health work in both South Africa and South America, and was about to leave on an expedition into the heart of Africa when he died in London. He was decorated by the King of Belgium, and during his last illness he was knighted by King George V of England.

At the command of the British king, Gorgas was given a state funeral with full military honors at London's historic Saint Paul's Cathedral. He received honorary degrees from many universities, and meritorious medals from many nations. He now lies in Arlington National Cemetery. Thus it is proper and befitting that the Gorgas Home should be made a state shrine in his memory, and maintained by the state for posterity to know more about William Crawford Gorgas, the world's greatest sanitarian.

On March 24, 1828, William Nichols, architect, submitted to the state legislature estimates and a plan for the University of Alabama. Included in that group of buildings was the present Gorgas Home, built in 1829. It was an ambitious plan, and had many similarities to the one Jefferson designed for the University of Virginia. The rotunda, with its twenty-four encircling columns, was the finest of the numerous buildings and was placed in the center of the quadrangle. Other buildings included Washington and Jefferson Colleges, and Madison and Franklin dormitories. Unfortunately, all of these were burned by Federal troops during the Civil War.

However, if the two beautiful buildings which today remain as part of the Nichols contribution—the President's Mansion and the Gorgas Home—are patterns to judge from, then one can but begin to visualize the imposing campus that it must have been. The Gorgas Home was first used as a boarding hall, or dining hall for university students. It later was used as a hospital and also a postoffice, and prior to receiving its present name, it was called Stewart's Hall and also University Commons.

The Gorgas Home has been influential on the scene of American architecture. Pictures and references to it are found repeatedly in books of Greek Revival and early American architecture. This is due no doubt to its high order, its stateliness, and its sensitive delineation of simple elegance. It is built of red brick taken from the fifty acres, highly conducive to brick-making, and purchased by the university founders for that purpose, which lay adjacent to the campus. Fortunately, it has never been stuccoed, and the beauty of the handmade brick is still to be seen.

The plan of the house is similar to the President's Mansion, only less of the grand manner. The ground floor has a sitting room, office, dining room, serving room—the kitchen was built separately and to the rear, and the first floor has a parlor and three bedrooms.

The raised portico is a lovely thing of much beauty. The ground floor porch has four brick pillars, connected at the top by flat arches. These support the Doric order of four fluted columns on the first floor. And winding down sandstone steps on either side of the first floor veranda, are decorative balustrades of ornamental iron. The same pattern of iron-grille extends across the veranda, connecting with the balustrades of the stairs, thus forming a highly creative touch of architectural unity and grace and over-all completeness.

The setting itself is picturesque. In the lawn stands the rugged "Gorgas Oak," now estimated to be nearing 350 years of age, which is quite remarkable itself for a water oak in north Alabama. Ever since General Josiah Gorgas moved into the house in 1879, members of his family have lived there. And even until this day, descendants remain, it now being occupied by General Gorgas's two daughters, Miss Bayne Gorgas and Mrs. George Palfrey, and his granddaughter, Mrs. Jessie Leake.

The Gorgas Home has been influential on the scene of American architecture due to its high order, its stateliness, and its sensitive delineation of simple elegance.

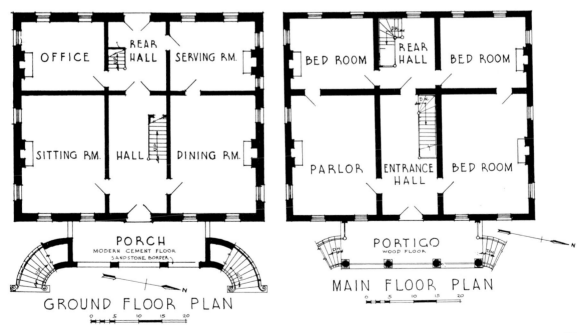

89

Gorgas Home. These decorative balustrades of ornamental iron wind down sandstone stairs on both sides of the raised portico.

90

THE GOVERNOR'S MANSION, Tuscaloosa, Alabama

Tuscaloosa, with its broad, treelined avenues, has one of the state's most handsomely planned residential sections. And taking its place in the very foremost vantage spot of all the many early mansions in the city, is the beautiful old mansion known today as the Governor's Mansion.

The house was built by Captain James Hunter Dearing, the riverboat captain who piloted the first steamboat from Mobile to Tuscaloosa. Histories record several dates for the building of the house. However, these seem to be the facts: the state legislature on March 2, 1819, the very day that Alabama became a state, gave to the proposed University of Alabama, the land upon which the Governor's Mansion stands; said land was to be used or sold for the purpose of raising funds for the new University.

On January 1, 1834, Captain Dearing purchased a small tract of the land for his house and estate which extended from University Avenue to Fourth Street and from Queen City Avenue to Pinehurst Avenue. He immediately set about building a mansion of quality and lasting beauty. It was probably finished in 1835. It is not known what architect was employed to design the house, but one is led strongly to believe that an architect, with ideas deft and facile, must have drawn plans for the mansion, so exacting are its dimensions and so masterfully perfected are its many details.

Tuscaloosa had some thirty-five mansions built during the two lush decades from 1826-46 when the state capital was located there, and yet the Governor's Mansion maintains an eminence of individuality and good architecture which has stood the test of time and decay, while others of the mansions have faltered by the wayside.

The house was built on an incline and faces down the city's main business thoroughfare, and directly beyond, to what was once the front of the old state capitol building. Thus, it is only natural that this mansion was one day destined to be lived in by a governor.

The mansion has a gently sloping hipped roof, a plain entablature, and six very fine Ionic columns. Even as fine as the columns are, it is the double doors, upstairs and down, which add the architect's finest touch to the portico. For here are found exceedingly fine entrances, with elliptical transoms. Numerous mansions have one such fine transom, but here are two, both of exquisite quality and done by expert craftsmen. A balcony with crow-foot balusters overhangs the porch entrance. The balustrade which once surrounded the Widow's Walk of the roof has since been removed, and pleasingly so. In recent years a sun parlor was added to the right front.

The interior of the mansion maintains the same high quality of workmanship as does the exterior. Of special interest is its beautiful staircase and the spacious parlors.

Captain Dearing soon grew weary of living in his new house. The rear of the estate was very close to the new University and adventurous students took to robbing his chicken houses, carrying away his bronze turkeys, and purloining his fruit before it was fully tree-ripened. This bothered the owner very much and on March 7, 1836, he sold the house and built himself another one, though not as fine, in the residential section that is now called Dearing Place.

The Governor's Mansion was bought by Richard H. Lewis, and he in turn sold it to Governor Arthur Pendleton Bagby on March 10, 1838. Bagby resided in the mansion from that time until he went out of office in 1841. He is the only governor who ever lived in the house.

During the same year that his term as governor ended, he was elected to the United States Senate where he served until his resignation, June 16, 1848. President James K. Polk then appointed him Envoy Extraordinary and Minister Plenipotentiary to Russia's Court of St. Petersburg. He resigned when President Zachary Taylor was elected, but was succeeded by another eminent Alabamian, William Rufus King, who was later elected Vice President of the United States. Bagby later lived in Camden and Mobile and was the father of nine children.

The Governor's Mansion then passed through some half dozen ownerships before finally being given to the University of Alabama. It is now a faculty club, used for rest, recreation and entertainment of faculty members. It is ironical that this land, originally given to the University, should now return to it after having passed through such a long and illustrious line of owners. Certainly the mansion has never been in better hands, for University officials, through the generosity of Mr. and Mrs. H. D. Warner, have made it into the show place that it once was during the gala society days when Governor Bagby entertained so fashionably.

The Governor's Mansion. This Tuscaloosa house of quality came to be known as The Governor's Mansion after it was purchased in 1838 by Arthur Pendleton Bagby during his term as governor.

DEARING-SWAIM HOME, Tuscaloosa, Alabama

Two brothers built two mansions in Tuscaloosa which remain today as monuments to the high perfection of Greek Revival architecture in Alabama. James Dearing built the house known as the Governor's Mansion, and Alexander B. Dearing built what is generally known today as the Swaim Home.

This Swaim Home was built during 1835-37 by slaves brought from Alexander B. Dearing's plantation near Columbus, Mississippi. The clay holes from which the bricks were made can still be seen about one mile from town on the Greensboro Road. No doubt Mr. Dearing was attracted to Tuscaloosa by family ties and also by the sudden influx of socially and politically prominent people who desired to locate in the state capital city. Mr. Dearing lived in his mansion until near the end of the Civil War when he died of "swamp fever."

One of his daughters married Dr. William S. Wyman, four times acting president of the University of Alabama, and they lived in the old house for many years after the builder died. It then passed to Mr. and Mrs. James S. Spence, and in 1919 it was purchased by the S. G. Swaim family who maintain it today in a fashionable and loving manner.

For years the Swaim Home has repeatedly been referred to as the "most perfect example of Greek Revival architecture in Tuscaloosa," and certainly it is one of the finest such examples in the entire state. Sixteen Ionic columns extend around three sides of the house, making it, next to Forks of Cypress which has columns on all four sides, the exemplar temple type mansion in Alabama.

The mansion is further enhanced by the spacious and well kept grounds, and is one of the most charming and beautiful of all the old homes featured during the annual spring pilgrimage in Tuscaloosa.

The Dearing-Swaim Home, with its sixteen beautiful Ionic columns extending around three sides of the house, is one of the two finest temple-like mansions in Alabama.

94

CHEROKEE, Tuscaloosa, Alabama

One of the last grand manner mansions built in Alabama during the decade before the Civil War cast its gray gloom over the region, was Cherokee, the home of Robert Jemison of Tuscaloosa.

It significantly reflects the desire for a new expression, a new splurge in the realm of architecture. For here is a complete turning away from the forty-year domination in Tuscaloosa, as well as Alabama, of the Greek Revival. Gone are the white pillars, the classic pediments, the fret and acanthus trimming. It might well have been the builder's whim to be different, and then again, it might have been the result of a more deep seated longing: a completely new architecture to express the changing times, the moving ahead, and the impending decadence.

Anyway, Jemison sent to Philadelphia for an architect by the name of Lewis and had him to execute plans for his sumptuous mansion of twenty-six rooms. No architect ever found a more abundant supply of building materials, as well as skilled assistants in the frontier days, than were provided by the Jemisons.

If ever a financial family dynasty was created in early Alabama, it was by William Jemison, the father of Robert. A man of broad talent, keen business initiative, and wise in the handling of men—Jemison carried on a vast business enterprise which included coal mining, stage coach operation, road construction, an extensive lumber and sawmill operation, iron ore smelting, as well as maintaining huge plantations. And it was he who built the first bridge across the Black Warrior River at Tuscaloosa.

And because he was wise in handling men, he grouped his many slaves according to their skill, their industriousness, and their ability to learn new things—an intellectual division. And then he set about teaching the most able group the arts of carpentry, stonecutting, moulding, masonry, brick-making, and artisan work in general. History records that many of these slaves reached high degrees of skill, so much so that while not busily engaged for the Jemisons themselves, they were hired to others who were building mansions, public buildings, or other types of construction. Jemison's was the most enterprising and ambitious operation of training and hiring skilled slave labor that the state ever had.

Thus, when Robert decided to build a commodious mansion in the already mansion studded city of Tuscaloosa, he had a talented reservoir of skilled artisans to draw from, and these were able, under proper supervision, to execute Lewis's architectural drawings fully and in minute detail.

However, this was not the first house called Cherokee by the Jemisons. William Jemison years before, when the region was still populated by Indians, had built a mansion a few miles northwest of Tuscaloosa as the cultural center of his four-thousand acre plantation. And he called it Crab Orchard, but the name was later changed to Cherokee—Cherokee, a name which has continued down through all the generations of Jemisons which have followed. The name memorialized a Cherokee chieftain and his tribe which saved Senator Robert Jemison's wife's parents—the Greenberry Taylors —from a Choctaw bushwacking, scalping escapade in which the Taylors and their neighbors' houses were burned and many of the whites massacred. According to a pledge with the Cherokee chieftain, the Taylors' next baby girl was to be named Cherokee, and it was she who became the senator's wife.

Senator Jemison's new home on Greensboro Avenue contained twenty-six rooms, many of them exceedingly large, and the grandest of which were the double parlors, eighteen feet in height and of the finest quality of carpentry, moulding and design.

The newel post and balusters of the delicate spiral staircase were carved from walnut and light oak, with a touch of inlaid chinaberry. A large basement was planned for entertainment and had a ball room, billiard room, game room, wine cellar, as well as dressing rooms—all of which were highly functional for the sumptuous entertaining that the owner loved so well. There was also a furnace and a plant for making gas from coal. The kitchen and cooking department was located in the basement of a wing which jutted out from the main body of the house. The prepared food was hoisted up a dumb-waiter to the serving room above, and then carried into the adjoining dining room.

The mansion is designed in the Italianate manner. No doubt the Jemisons had come under the influence of the great Italian villas which had begun to impress more and more Americans as they journeyed to Italy to view its wonders, its climate, its architecture.

The ambitious three-sided first floor veranda is bordered with a whole galaxy of thin, square colonettes, the opening between each group of posts being arched in fancy wood-carved, open work tracery. This arch effect is carried out further in the Palladian door with sidelights on the small observation porch of the second floor. The house is crowned with a square observation tower, with eight tall multi-paned windows on all four sides, as well as a suggested pedimental effect. A miniature steeple rises from the very apex of the cupola roof.

Cherokee is one of the two finest Italianate mansions in Alabama, the other being Kendall Manor in Eufaula. Cherokee has recently been magnificently restored by the J. P. Burchfields, after having been in sad neglect for many years. It is one of the show places on the old homes pilgrimage held each spring in Tuscaloosa.

Cherokee, in Tuscaloosa, Robert Jemison's mansion, is one of the two finest Italianate mansions in the state.

CHAPTER IV

The Black Belt Region

Eutaw	Greensboro
Near Forkland	Marion
Demopolis	Uniontown
Selma	

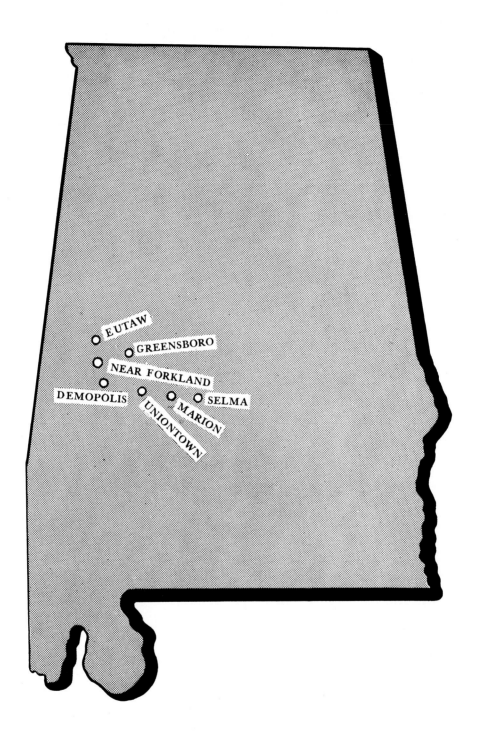

(The Black Belt Region)

THE BANKS HOME, Eutaw, Alabama

The Banks Home in Eutaw was built in 1854 by James Oliver Banks, and has remained, along with a fine collection of heirloom antiques, in the Banks family ever since.

The massing of its fluted Ionic columns, its fenestration, and the heavy boldness of its pilastered, sidelighted entrances, and the full veranda length of its overhanging balcony—all of these make it a town house of unusually fine proportions and enduring charm. The queen of Eutaw's more than two dozen ante-bellum mansions, the Banks Home has been maintained with fastidious care.

KIRKWOOD, Eutaw, Alabama

Kirkwood was finished in 1860 and it bears a constant reminder that the war was at hand, a war which was to leave its imprint upon the mansion until this very day, because the ornamental iron ordered for the veranda balcony was caught up in the sweep of the war and never came. So today the balcony is there and is still without the iron railing.

The house does however verify the fact that Greek Revival was still very much in vogue in Alabama right up to the outbreak of the war.

Kirkwood was built by Foster M. Kirksey, a planter and merchant who settled in Eutaw in 1839. It has remained in the Kirksey family since the beginning, and is today owned by Dr. H. A. Kirksey.

The veranda here is an energetic use of the Greek Revival, in that the builder was not satisfied with a simple façade; he extended it across the front and then down the west side, making an expansive portico half way around the house. The eight free-standing columns are of the fluted Ionic with egg and dart motif featured on the capitals. The cornice brackets of the entablature, not being Greek, distract somewhat from the otherwise classic façade. The originally designed cupola with columns has been reduced to a low-standing menial one, however this does not take from the panoramic view of the house since the cupola, as well as much of the house itself, is hidden by the spreading oaks, magnolias, cedars and mimosa trees.

The entrance doors are similar to others found in Eutaw homes and probably were made by the same carpenter. They have sidelights of multi-colored glass and very broad doorheads, without transoms. The windows opening onto the veranda extend fully to the floor; and the windows, as well as the entranceway, have supporting pilasters on either side with egg and dart capitals.

The most unusual feature about the entire portico is the whip-sawn pine timber fitted to the sidings with a plasterlike finish without the use of tongue and groove. The lasting beauty of this timber is indicative of the quality workmanship on the carpenters part. This same high quality is reflected in the interior woodwork which is referred to as the seven coat woodwork—meaning that it was finished with seven different coats of paint. It has remained in such superb condition that it has never been necessary to repaint it. The plastering also is in its fine original state, as are the floors.

Of the numerous marble mantels in the mansion, the one in the drawing room is the most beautiful. Of white Carrara marble, the mantel is lavishly carved with the goddesses of the seasons. Spring has the carving of a young girl's head, surrounded with flowers in relief. For summer the goddess is shown with wheat and corn. A horn-of-plenty filled with the season's harvest denotes the goddess of fall.

The interior of the mansion has many charming points of interest: the walnut staircase, the marble top shelves between the drawing room windows, the marble mantel with the angel's head, the rosewood piano, the fiddleback chairs. But as one goes from room to room it is always the magnificent quality of workmanship that attracts the connoisseur's eye.

It is with a note of regret that the final touches of resplendent finesse were never added, due to the war—the iron-grille balcony, the crystal chandeliers, the brass and-irons. And yet, perhaps it is the very absence of these which gives the visitor the authentic recording of what the war actually did for the building and finishing of mansions in the South.

Kirkwood was finished in 1860 on the eve of the Civil War. The ornamental iron ordered for the balcony never came—it was stopped somewhere by the shipping blockade.

ROSEMOUNT, near Forkland, Alabama

Like a beautiful white rose in radiant bloom, Rosemount—The Grand Mansion of Alabama—defies time and decay atop a commanding star-shaped hill where she has stood since 1832. It was here, in the heart of Alabama's rich Black Belt grazing land, that Williamson Allen Glover came when Alabama was only thirteen years old, and made for himself a magnificent mansion.

This masterfully conceived twenty-room mansion was designed and built by Glover, who reared his sixteen children in true elegance and splendor at Rosemount. Seven years and the help of dozens of slaves were required to hew the timber from the 3,000-acre Glover plantation; to mold and bake the thousands of brick that went into the foundation, the chimneys, and the long walkways; and to saw piece by piece the enormous amount of timber for the magnificent dwelling. Sheltered behind the great Ionic columns is the governor's balcony from which eagle eyes once kept watch on the numerous Glover belles as they were courted by swains from adjoining plantations.

A large reception hall, made friendly by a Grandfather Clock ticking away the time, opens on either side into two sweeping parlors—one a gentlemen's parlor, and the other for the ladies. The ladies' parlor is filled with the most finery, for there is found the rosewood piano, a giant *etagère* loaded with Bisque figurines, Wedgwood vases, and Wheeling peachblow vases; early American primitive paintings; and a Dolly Madison mirror above the black Carrara marble mantel brought from Italy. And on the mantel is a pair of silver candlesticks encased within large etched and cut hurricane shades, and centering the mantel is a set of Paul and Virginia Girandole candelabra. Resting on a marble-topped table is a huge French Buhl clock of brass and ebony.

The great transverse hall extending sixty feet across the house was the scene of musicales, hoop-skirt dancing and gala receptions. The toddy room was just at the end where gentlemen partook of spirits, since in those early days Southern gentlemen never drank in the presence of ladies.

The table of the Empire banquet set, used in Rosemount since it was built, opens to seat twenty-four dinner guests in the state dining room, decorated on either end by gleaming white marble mantels imported from Italy.

The bride's room, which once was the master's bedroom, is graced by an Adamlike mantel. An exquisitely handcarved French rosewood suite of furniture lends a rare elegance to the room. The wardrobe of the set, lined with birdseye maple, has expandable hoop-skirt shelves, and a false drawer in the bottom.

Another great hall commands space and attention in the center of the second story where it is surrounded by six bedrooms, furnished with massive tester beds, one of which has a convenient blanket-roll at the foot where the blanket is wrapped until need in the cool of night.

104

It seems that no spot in the entire house registers quite the lasting impression on visitors as does the wing-back *acouchement* chair. When its padded seat is lifted, there below, is revealed a round cut-out hole where slave-attended masters once sat for convenience, and beneath the opening was placed a fancy chamber from the nearby mahogany chamber closet. For many years this secret convenience was hidden in the chair and it was not until recently when it was being reupholstered that its utility value was once again revealed.

The crowning beauty of Rosemount is the thirty-by-fifteen foot cupola atop the mansion. From its colonnaded walkway the Glover masters used to keep an eye telescoped upon the work of their slaves as they tilled the bountiful acres. From here also they watched their privately chartered steamboats ferry their own cotton away to Liverpool in distant England.

Rosemount has recently undergone a complete restoration inside and out, as a result of having passed into new ownership after being in the Glover family for more than a hundred years. The new owners, Mr. and Mrs. Edward DeVesci, have done a remarkable job, in that they themselves have done the actual work, including the plastering, papering, reupholstering and refinishing of the floors and woodwork. Done as a hobby, the two of them executed the entire job with excellent craftsmanship. It is their plan also to restore the long neglected formal garden, now overgrown with giant boxwood, camellias, and massive magnolias.

Exceptionally fine points of architecture are found in the following: (1) the handsomely executed fluted columns with superlative Ionic capitals; (2) the identically fashioned doorways on each of the three story entrances—sidelights and transom on the main floor are of ruby Bohemian glass, bearing crystal patterns of flowers and vines; (3) the most elaborate cupola in the entire state; and (4) the magnificent woodwork of the four double doors in the large entrance vestibule.

Rosemount is one of the few ante-bellum mansions in Alabama in which the original furnishings have remained with the house. The library, clothes, keys, and even the children's toys are still there. All of this of course adds much to the over-all charm and interest of the mansion.

For a number of years now Rosemount has been open daily to visitors. And that is significant, because it is an ante-bellum mansion in Alabama where people can go, without reluctance, and see for themselves the way of life, as nearly as possible, as it was lived during the golden days of the Old South.

Rosemount, widely known as the Grand Mansion of Alabama, has the finest cupola, not only in Alabama, but in the entire Southland.

Rosemount. Williamson Allen Glover, the builder, reared sixteen children in his great house. Thus it is a foregone conclusion that a lot of living was done in the double parlors, one of which is shown here.

Rosemount. The banquet hall table will accommodate twenty-four guests. The room has two Carrara marble mantels. A pair of exquisitely etched hurricane shades decorate the table; another pair are on the buffet in the background.

Rosemount. This fine Adam-like mantel, with "gossip" chairs alongside, is in the bride's room. The French candelabra and clock have Sevres porcelain inlay.

108

THORNHILL, near Forkland, Alabama

Had the ancient Greeks come to Alabama in search of another Acropolis, they would have found at Thornhill the perfect spot to build their temples. Of all the ante-bellum homes in Alabama, Thornhill is the most handsomely situated atop a beautiful knoll overlooking thousands of acres of broad meadows and wooded forests extending in every direction. It is little wonder that such a place of beauty was immediately recognized as a choice homesite by young James Innes Thornton, that day in the early 1820's as he journeyed by horseback from his new law office in Huntsville down to Cahaba, the state capital.

Young Thornton had been reared in the elegance of Virginia aristocracy at Fall Hill, the Thornton plantation home on the banks of the Rappahanock, one mile from Fredericksburg. Upon completion of his law study at what is now Washington and Lee University, he joined the trek to the West where the adventure of the wilderness beckoned.

Thornton bought the broad acres upon first sight, and the austere brick house that was then located where the mansion was later to rise. Settling upon the place, he married Mary Ann Glover, daughter of Williamson Allen Glover who lived at Rosemount, a neighboring plantation. The union was shortlived. Mrs. Thornton died after the birth of her second child.

A second marriage soon followed; this time to his Virginia childhood sweetheart, Ann Amelia Smith, whose father had by now moved on to Mobile where he had entered the cotton business. It was shortly after this marriage that plans for the building of Thornhill commenced. The place took its name after the Thornton ancestral home, Thorn-on-the-Hill in England.

A man of considerable means, Mr. Thornton brought carpenters from Virginia, and sent slaves into his own forests to cut and saw the cypress, oak, pine and cedar which went into the building of this splendid mansion. It was finished in 1833. Its broad lines are strictly classic revival, adhering in every aspect to the finest points of Greek architecture. The six massive fluted Ionic columns line a handsome veranda, the view from which is unequalled as one looks out for miles over two counties.

The interior is not unlike the plan embodied in the construction of many another Alabama mansion. An exceptionally broad hall, upstairs and down, separates the equal proportions of two large rooms on either side of the hall. Upon entering the mansion, one is immediately struck by the grace of the circular staircase with its rich mahogany banister, spiralling upward at the far end of the hall.

The entire house is furnished in fine antiques, many of them having been shipped by water from Fall Hill via the Atlantic and the Gulf to Mobile and up the rivers to Thornhill. The rosewood and mahogany tester beds are of the best of their period, and are today in excellent condition, having been treated kindly by the dozens of children who romped and played and grew up at Thornhill.

In the upstairs hall hangs one of the original hand-drawn Snedecor maps of Greene County. Only twelve of these maps were made and less than half are now in existence. Unusual too is the Sleepy Hollow chair which adjusts its hidden mechanism so as to fit the size and shape of all who sit in it. Charm also is added by the silver doorknobs and fobs on the great sliding doors between the drawing room and the dining hall.

A kindred heritage which no other ante-bellum family in Alabama can match, is the Thornton connection with General George Washington and the priceless heirlooms which came down to Thornhill through this relationship. There is a brass candleholder which once belonged to Nellie Custis, and a giant cup and saucer frequently used at Mount Vernon by the great general himself. But the most cherished family possession, hanging in the hall for all to see, is the telescope used by Washington and given by him to Francis Thornton—grandfather of the present Thornhill master— who was an aide to General Washington during the Revolutionary War.

The relationship of the Thornton and Washington families dates back to the mid-1700's when Francis Thornton II married Frances Gregory, whose mother, Mildred Washington Gregory, was the only sister of Augustine Washington, the father of George Washington. Mildred Washington was not only the general's aunt, but also his God-mother, upon whom it is reported the Godchild lavished much affection.

Another historic heirloom which came in later years to Thornhill is the elaborate set of goldbanded china once owned by Queen Charlotte of England. It was inherited by Butler Brayne Spottswood Thornton from her father, The Duke of Ormond, who came into possession of it while serving in the British court.

Thornhill's first master was elected Alabama's Secretary of State in 1824 and served for ten years. It was his distinct honor to be the state's official escort for the great La-Fayette when he visited Alabama in 1825. Thornton met LaFayette at the Georgia border and accompanied him on to the capital at Cahaba, as well as on an extensive tour of the entire state. It is interesting to note that records kept by the Secretary reveal that Alabama spent $17,000.00 on the entertainment of the French guest.

The first master's brother, Harry Innes Thornton—father of James Innes Thornton II, present owner of Thornhill—also led an illustrious public life, having been a member of the Supreme Court of Alabama, and appointed by President Franklin Pierce as the first Federal Land Commissioner of California.

Today, Thornhill is much like it was a hundred years ago. The Lombardy oaks, grown from slips taken from the mother trees at Fall Hill, are becoming sturdier with age. The present owner, now in his seventies, has retained the natural beauty of the home and the surroundings. Nothing is changed except the new faces of Thorntons who come with each generation.

Somehow, one has the feeling that James Innes Thornton I, who lies buried there beside the house, is happy with the way later Thorntons have loved and cared for Thornhill, which itself is a proud monument to him whose headstone reads:

"In my hand no price I bring,
Simply to Thy Cross I cling."

110

Thornhill, built by a cousin of George Washington, is situated on a high hilltop with a view of two counties stretching out across the meadows and woodlands below.

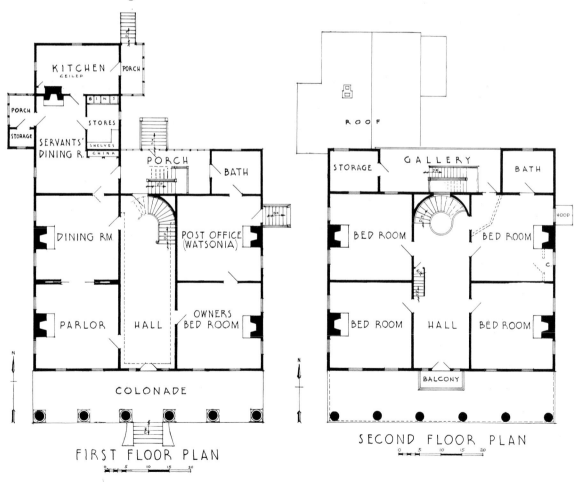

111

The master cup and saucer, the candleholder, and the telescope were handed down from the Washington family. The telescope was used by George Washington when he worked as a surveyor during his young days.

Thornhill. The family schoolhouse, located on the front lawn, followed the classic lines of the nearby mansion. During the Civil War it was used as a sewing place where Confederate garments were made.

Thornhill. Family heirlooms decorate the central hall, with spiral staircase.

Thornhill. The pier mirror and the family portrait over the mantel lend a touch
of dignity to the comfortable dining room with rich Oriental rug.

113

GAINESWOOD, Demopolis, Alabama

There are more than two thousand ante-bellum mansions in Alabama today, yet Gaineswood, the Whitfield home in Demopolis, "is the most magnificent of all," according to E. Walter Burkhardt, professor of architecture who directed the Historic American Buildings Survey of historic Alabama homes. Here at Gaineswood is the glorification of the Greek Revival—the glorified embodiment of the finest as exemplified in the Neo-Classic.

While the builders of other lavish mansions in Alabama's Black Belt were striving to reproduce as nearly as possible identical likenesses of the Greek temples, there developed at Gaineswood a rare exception. The builder used the same motifs, the same materials, and even the same architectural handbooks from which the orders were developed, yet a new beauty, a new conception of the fullest possibilities of Greek Revival architecture resulted in the building of Gaineswood. Commenting on this point, Howard Major, writing in his *Domestic Architecture of the Early American Republic*, states, "An interesting exception to the general arrangement is Gaineswood . . . the composition, a main body with subsidiary wings and porches, was carefully studied, and the result is successful and interesting from all four sides."

General Nathan Bryan Whitfield, the builder of Gaineswood, had a distinguished ancestry dating back many centuries. Whitfield Hall, his family's ancestral home, was built on the West Allen River in Northumberland, long before that region became a part of England. While the construction date of Whitfield Hall is unknown, it is conservative to surmise that it dates back to the eleventh century, for Sir Thomas Whitfield, nineteenth in descent in the mediaeval manor, in 1606, became head of the East India Company. The builder of Gaineswood was twenty-fifth in descent. His illustrious father, General Bryan Whitfield, was one of the founders of the University of North Carolina at Chapel Hill. This brilliant scion of the North Carolina family, and his two brothers, Needham and Paul, made outstanding military records during the Revolutionary War—all three having participated in the battle of Moore's Creek in eastern North Carolina in 1776.

Before migrating west to Alabama, Gaineswood's first master distinguished himself by serving both in the North Carolina House of Commons and later in the North Carolina Senate. Any political aspirations he might have had in Alabama, no doubt, were thwarted by his zealous determination to see the fruition of his dreams, Gaineswood, brought to completion—a task which consumed a decade and a half of his energy.

Born in 1799, General Whitfield made his first trip to Marengo County, Alabama, in 1833 when he came to visit his uncle, Colonel J. R. Bryan, who had settled there in 1821. General Whitfield was so impressed with the possibilities of the 'Horn of Plenty' way of life in Alabama, that he purchased a plantation consisting of several thousand

114

acres which he called Chatham. The location was fifteen miles from Demopolis. As his slaves began to transform the forests into productive fields, the master began to make friends with neighboring settlers. His most ardent friend was found in General George S. Gaines, Choctaw Indian factor whose headquarters were at Fort Tombeckbe, later called Fort Confederation, on the Tombigbee River in Sumter County. It was his brother, Captain Edmund Gaines, who captured renegade Aaron Burr, near McIntosh, Alabama, when the former vice-president was being sought as a traitor to his country.

By 1842 the Choctaws had succumbed to the onrush of the whites, and there was no longer any need of such an outpost as had been maintained by General Gaines. It was at this time that Whitfield purchased fifteen hundred acres of land on the outskirts of Demopolis from Gaines. The tract included the log house which had been the home of the Indian agent. In fact, the giant oak tree, estimated to be 350 years old and still standing there beside the main entrance to Gaineswood, was the spot where Gaines signed the treaty with Chief Pushmataha which provided for the removal west of the Choctaw Nation. Whitfield moved to his new land from Chatham, razed the log cabin, and in its stead began to build Gaineswood, naming it in honor of his faithful friend, General Gaines.

Nathan Bryan Whitfield was by no means the most colorful newcomer welcomed to Demopolis by the Indian factor. In 1818 there came to the region the most picturesque band of immigrants ever to set foot in Alabama. They were Napoleonic refugees fleeing from the courts of France after their benefactor and idol was exiled to Elba. This group was led by Count Lefebvre-Desnouettes, Napoleon's most trusted companion. A general in the French army, it was Desnouettes who rode in Napoleon's own snow sled during the retreat from Moscow; and it was to Desnouettes whom the Little Corporal administered the customary French cheek-kiss goodbye when he bade farewell to his faithful military guard before departing from Fontainebleu into exile.

This strange entourage consisted of many romantic figures: among others equally worthy of mention were Count Nicholas Raoul and his wife, the former Marchioness of Sinbaldi who had been lady-in-waiting to the Queen of France; M. Peniers, Republican leader of the French National Assembly under Louis XIV; Count Bernard Clausel; and Lieutenant Henri L'Allemand. They brought with them their Brussels carpets, their satin shoes and brocaded train-flowing gowns. Their purpose was to establish a Vine and Olive Colony in the New World. Men plowed the fields in generals' uniforms, women prepared the food in gowns which they had formerly worn to serve queens. In a few short years the venture failed. The wilderness was too great for the noblemen to conquer. However there are today olive trees and grapevines in Demopolis which were planted by these very people. And, too, there are a few French names found today in Marengo County—descendants of those few colonists who were determined to turn failure into success.

It was when the colony project failed that squatters and wealthy settlers from the Carolinas and Virginia rushed in and bought up the land which the Frenchmen had cleared and made ready for cultivation. And it was at this time that Nathan Bryan Whitfield came to this region of Alabama referred to as the 'Canebrake,' to build his house, Gaineswood.

While plantation owners newly arrived throughout the region were bringing in skilled artisans and novice artisans to frame designs for country houses, General Whitfield depended entirely upon his own ability. In his library, extensive for its time, the general studied the various handbooks of architecture which were the main source of inspiration for the Neo-Classic builders. He executed in exacting detail the cornices and elaborate columns depicted in the handbooks. A surviving grandson now in his 90's, Jesse Whitfield, has in his possession a Bielefield catalogue from which the plaster castings were taken, as well as a set of *The Antiquities of Athens* by Stuart and Revett. He states that his grandfather used these and Vitruvius's work as guides for the decorations.

The builder of Gaineswood was a practical man. Once knowing the rough plan and the massing of the structure, he set to work building carpentry and plaster shops on the premises. He even designed and made the lathes and pieces of intricate machinery which were used to fashion the columns and the cornices. Power for the whirling lathes was supplied by an eight-mule team which revolved circuitously around a gear shaft, which itself was the handiwork of the general. Batter houses and brick kilns also sprang up nearby. It was in these shops that the mechanical ability of Whitfield showed to best advantage, for it was here that his aesthetic dreams became reality.

The main entrance to the house is through the *porte cochere,* facing west, which opens onto the circular driveway winding up from the iron gate. Jesse Whitfield tells that when the general was about to put into place a plaster medallion on the ceiling of the *porte cochere,* a Polish vagabond happened by, exhibited his handiwork, and as a result, the general hired him to paint a wreath of flowers—"the most beautiful fresco I have ever seen," Whitfield said, to replace the plaster medallion.

Another entrance opens onto the north veranda which is the front of the house. The veranda, although narrow, is beautified by two rows of supporting posts, the inner being square and of stone and concrete, while the outer row is of wood, rounded and fluted. All are of simple Doric design. The stone wall of the house directly behind the portico was originally lined off into retangular blocks, an architectural device widely used at the time, and the blocks were then marbelized with veins of grayish blue interlacing the lighter background.

The veranda faces an enclosed formal garden, called on the original plans, the north *parterre.* A similar one faces south on the opposite side of the house. The original cypress blocks enclosing the *parterres* have been replaced by stone.

The general's baby daughter, Mrs. Nathalie Whitfield Winn, now ninety, says that she remembers the intricate patterns of the gardens flowering in sweet olive, hyacinth, buttercups, kiss-me-at-the-gate, flowering quince, bridal wreath, and roses that included Cloth of Gold, Marschal Neil, Jacques Minot, Etoile de Lyon, Lady Banksia, and Malmaison. The Dancing Girl, a life size marble statue by the Italian sculptor, Canova, which once stood in the center of the north *parterre,* has since been removed, along with other of the statuary which graced the grounds. The Dancing Girl, and another of Canova's pieces, Pamona, Goddess of Fruit, were copies of originals which had been executed for the Empress Josephine. These, along with several other statues, can be seen today on lawns of Demopolis homes where Whitfield descendants live.

The stone slabs at the bottom of the steps leading into the north *parterre* came as ballast on a cotton boat from Scotland.

Inside the double doors of the *porte cochere,* one enters a long hall, with a reception room on either side. The elaborate marble mantels of these rooms were removed during a time of decay and neglect. To the left of the hall is the drawing room, Gaineswood's most magnificent chamber, and to the right, the parlor. From the far end of the hall, one enters the master's room, and beyond it, through a hall, the mistress's room.

The drawing room is one of the most lavish and spectacular rooms in any private residence in the nation. Twenty by thirty feet in size, the room has at either end identical gray marble mantels, with wreathed rosettes decorating the head slabs. Lining the long axial walls are exquisite fluted pilasters and midway along each wall is found a recess, into which a vis-a-vis mirror is fitted with exacting parallelism. These mirrors, shipped from France, afford a magnificent spectacle in that they provide thirteen reflections and counter-reflections as one looks into each. The mirrors were once glorified in true Grecian splendor by a statue of Flora and another of Ceres mounted before them. These now belong to Jesse Whitfield. The twin mirrors over the mantels have been removed. One is in the possession of Mrs. Winn and the other is owned by Asa Whitfield, the builder's nephew.

An artist whom members of the family believe to be the Pole who painted the fresco, decorated the panels beside the vis-a-vis mirrors, as well as other sectional panels in the room, with clusters of fruit. These were painted in their natural colors, and Mrs. Winn says they showed "peaches, pomegranate, apples, pears and plums," and that they looked "real enough to eat."

The ceiling of the room is fashioned in protruding sections of cross-beams, all highly embossed with plaster designs. The interlacing of the beams form deep coffers; each of which is studded with dainty rosettes. The Corinthian order throughout the room is taken from the Choragic Monument of Lysicrates at Athens. A rinceau acanthus frieze was substituted for the one of the Greek monument.

The general's daughter tells of the early balls held in this room, with friendly Indians still living in the vicinity, peering curiously through the windows to see the Virginia Reel and the minuet being performed.

When fencing artists came from France to teach swordsmanship to the Whitfield boys, the chandelier and the mirrors were wrapped and boarded, and spectators stood in the doors and the windows watching the fencing movements.

This room is the scene of one of the unique stories about Gaineswood, a story which gives insight into the time required for its construction. In 1855, Mrs. Winn relates, when her oldest brother was to be married, the wall of the drawing room next to the hall had not been completed, so her father, man of clever practicality that he was, ordered from Mobile a sheet of canvas thirty feet long, and painted the wall with its columns, cornices, mirrors and all, and stretched it into position. "The job was so perfect," Mrs. Winn states, "that when the wedding took place, only a few of the guests noted that it was a painting." From this incident is established the fact that the house was not completed by 1855. Mrs. Winn says that it was finished about 1860—making a total of eighteen years spent on construction.

At the east end of the drawing room commences a transverse hall which extends thirty feet and thence into an entrance hall that opens onto the south porch. It is this porch which overlooks the south *parterre*. The transverse hall runs midway between the parlor, or library, and the dining room. In these chambers are found the most unique feature of the entire construction of Gaineswood. Both of the rooms have superbly fashioned domes, constructed by the builder as a main source of lighting.

Atop each dome is a circular cupola, three feet in diameter, jutting skyward far enough to allow for artistic spacing of lengthy windows. Originally the panes were of soft blue, but in later years they have been replaced with clear glass. Each of the window sections is separated by miniature columns of the Ionic order, while the base of the cupola is enhanced by large acanthus leaves, individually spaced. The plaster ornamentation of the domes is beautiful in its artistry of Greek honeysuckles, encased in flowing scrolls, each of which is crested with a tiny flower. From the top of the cupolas, chandeliers hang on long chains. Certainly this is one of the most brilliant achievements of layman craftsmanship ever executed in the ante-bellum South.

General Whitfield was a stickler when it came to carrying out his plans. His daughter tells how he journeyed to Mobile on a lengthy business trip, and upon returning, found that the parlor ceiling had been completed as a flat surface without the dome and cupola. He immediately ordered the ceiling removed to make way for his own design. A plaster artisan by the name of Vinson, from Philadelphia, who had been hired to assist the general in executing the plans, soon found that to deviate from the drawings meant a re-doing of the entire job.

The same honeysuckle pattern employed on the domes was also used on the door-heads and the pendants, only here castiron was used in lieu of plaster. The castiron was shipped from Philadelphia, and while it is not seen extensively in ante-bellum homes in Alabama, it is by no means a rarity. A gracefully executed bust of General George Washington is mounted atop the parlor door opening into the main hall. The doors in the parlor, as well as numerous others in the house, are topped with glass transoms bearing colorful mythological scenes such as Phoebus, God of Sun. Two of these, beaded with lead cames, are of the original Venetian glass, while others were broken by vandals when the house was unoccupied.

On either side of the entrance hall facing south are two small rooms on a lower floor level than the other rooms. The one to the left was a bedroom while the one to the right was used as the general's plantation office. It also served as headquarters for General Leonidas Polk, the fighting bishop of Louisiana, when his division of troops encamped at Demopolis in 1864. Polk had been a classmate of Whitfield's at North Carolina.

A small and entirely separate upstairs, over the two rooms just described, is reached by a stairway extending from the southern extremity of the transverse hall. These two bedrooms are in the form of a mezzanine and are much lower in height than the upstairs proper. The general planned this as the nursery, and here the children were kept in well lighted rooms, removed from the gay noises which so often permeated the rooms below. These rooms, and the two directly below, have wooden mantels, one of which is Adamlike. The nine other mantels throughout the house are of gray marble, all having been imported from Italy.

The main upstairs is entered from the graceful staircase rising in the main hall. Three bedrooms are spaciously massed for the utmost of comfort. From the upstairs hall, an unfinished staircase leads up to the roof observatory. Called 'The Ring,' the cupola is distinctively individual in that it has no cover. It is merely an observatory platform, encircled with a balustrade. The red cedar and the heart cypress wood used in the balusters was of such sturdiness that even today the preservation is extraordinary. In the evenings the master and his children often held musicales in 'The Ring.' Mrs.

118

Winn and other descendants state that 'The Ring' was not a part of the original plans, but that it was added by young Bryan Watkins Whitfield in the summer of 1849 while vacationing at home after graduating from the University of North Carolina.

The two most elaborate bedrooms in the house are the master's and the mistress's. It was in the master's room that Mrs. Winn, the general's thirteenth and only child by his second wife, was born. The general was so delighted with his new baby, the first in sixteen years, that he would get up during the night and light slivers of kindling wood to look at the child. The marble mantel in this room has a pair of small free standing Ionic columns as its decorative supports. A secret staircase, hidden by a paneled door, leads to the second floor chambers from this room.

Just beyond the master's room lies the magnificent mistress's room, fit in every detail to suit the exacting whims of a queen. The pilasters and columns bordering the alcove overlooking the lawn are of a modified, less elaborate Corinthian order, exquisitely executed, and patterned after those in The Tower of the Winds in Athens. The curved sofa made to order for this rounded bay, is now in the possession of Mrs. Winn. A small door opens onto the narrow balcony bay, beautified by six small Doric columns.

Boldly constructed cellars and storage bins are found beneath the main body of the house. Here were stored bountiful quantities of food to supply both the family and the slaves. While to the rear of the house stood the large smoke house which accommodated the three annual killings of pork, each of which, according to old records, averaged between 30,000 and 40,000 pounds of meat.

The grounds surrounding the house were originally of many acres and of such landscaping as would suggest a Gainesborough pastoral scene. The focal point of the expansive front ground was a lake dug by slaves. The lake was centered with two small islands where grew Normandy poplars, cedars, and crepe myrtle. Steel engravings of the grounds with the house in the background were made about 1860 by the renowned artist, John Sartain. Prints from these plates are now displayed in the Metropolitan Museum of Art in New York, as well as in the Philadelphia Art Museum. It is interesting to note the identity of the figures in Sartain's choice engraving. The tiny baby in the buggy is Mrs. Winn herself, she having been born in 1859. She is being pushed by Ann, her Negro nurse, and directly behind are strolling the general and his wife. Two older daughters are seated in the boat on the lake, and Moso, the houseboy, is shown fetching an umbrella.

Grandson Jesse Whitfield tells how he took the box in which the vis-a-vis mirrors had been shipped from Paris, caulked the seams, and made a boat complete with sidewheels and crankshaft. "I spent many happy hours in that scow," he said.

An eleven-hundred foot well supplied water for the lake. It also furnished running water for washing and bathing in the house. It was the first artesian well in the region, and according to Mrs. Winn, "The force of the bubbling water would support the weight of a goodly sized apple." In later years when numerous wells were dug farther down the incline, the pressure subsided and the water had to be drawn by windlass.

Still standing at its vantage spot on the grounds is the summer house or love temple which members of the family say was patterned from one designed for Marie Antoinette. The eight Corinthian columns have the same exquisite design as those used in the drawing room. A favorite spot for courting couples, the temple once had a dome, topped with a large pineapple which had been handcarved by the general himself. The dome has been replaced by a less pretentious roof and the pineapple is today displayed on the south *parterre*.

Gaineswood has not always fared so kindly at the hand of fate. The Civil War depleted the Whitfield fortune, and their mansion became almost a tumbled down mass of ghostliness. A mulberry tree grew through the floor and into the skylight of the domed dining hall. Goats slept in the drawing room. Vandals carried away the cutglass prisms of the fine chandeliers.

In 1896 the home was purchased by Mrs. Charles Dunstan, daughter of the builder, from the general's eldest son, Bryan Watkins Whitfield who had bought it from his father in 1868. She began the devoted task of restoring the mansion to its former beauty.

The house passed through several other ownerships before its purchase in 1946 by Dr. and Mrs. J. D. McLeod of Ohio. Dr. McLeod, a native Alabamian, returned to his home state to retire. The place was in a neglected condition when he bought it and more than two years of continuous work were required to restore it to the exquisite place of beauty which it is today.

Although Gaineswood is stripped of its original Chippendale furnishings and its marble statues, this detracts little from the beauty of the mansion. The house itself was, and is, the thing of importance. While the present furniture is not the original, it lends much beauty and refinement to Alabama's finest ante-bellum dwelling.

The building of Gaineswood alone is by no means General Whitfield's only claim to genius. He was a musician. He played the pianoforte, violin, bagpipe and harp. He invented a musical instrument called the flutina which was a combination of a pianoforte and an organ with music similar to a flute streaming from a cylinder, hence flutina. He was an artist. The oil portrait he did at the age of seventeen of his father shows remarkable talent, while his self-portrait carved with a pocket knife from white pine shows further artistic agility.

He was an engineer. He designed, surveyed and built an amazing canal, replete with locks, as a drainage system for the surrounding land. Previously mentioned has been his mechanical ingenuity in the invention of machinery, lathes, and power wheels which made possible the building of Gaineswood. He was an architect and a builder. Gaineswood is his lasting monument to these achievements.

He was a kindly man, a man about whom his thirteen children spoke devotedly and affectionately. His was a life of continuous learning of new things, not the least of which was distant traveling with frequent trips to Philadelphia at the pace of "forty miles by the light of a single day." From these trips always came ample additions to his already voluminous library.

Architects from any nations have come to marvel at his magnificent contribution to the finer buildings of the world. No doubt he would best be pleased with his baby daughter's description of Gaineswood: "the whole thing is a symphony—the proportions so perfect, the detail so in tune." And, as from the beginning, the purple velvet of Jacob's Ladders still bloom in scattered patches across the lawn with the coming of each Spring.

Gaineswood is the finest Greek Revival mansion in Alabama. Its builder, Nathan Bryan Whitfield, was also its architect.

Rear view of Gaineswood shows "The Ring" observatory and the enclosed formal garden which the builder called the south *parterre*.

121

The combination of fluted columns and square pillars is used effectively in Gaineswood's numerous porticoes.

View from the West shows the *porte cochere*, and to the right, the wing with the mezzanine nursery upstairs, and directly below in the corner room which was the office of General Leonidas Polk, the Fighting Bishop of Louisiana.

Gaineswood. The summer house has columns identical with those in the drawing room.

Gaineswood. The alcove in the mistress's bedroom has rich columniation. The two freestanding columns were adapted from the Tower of the Winds in Athens.

The twin domes add architectural dignity and rare individuality to Gaineswood. The bust of George Washington was planned as part of the original door.

Gaineswood, the drawing room, with its magnificent coffer ceiling and plaster trim, is one of the very finest rooms in all America.

Here in panoramic view, separated by the transverse hall, is the parlor and the dining room. The chandeliers hang from the two domes.

Gaineswood. The superb plasterwork of the domes is indicated in this close-up view.

Gaineswood. Miniature columns were spaced in a ring around the skylights of the domes.

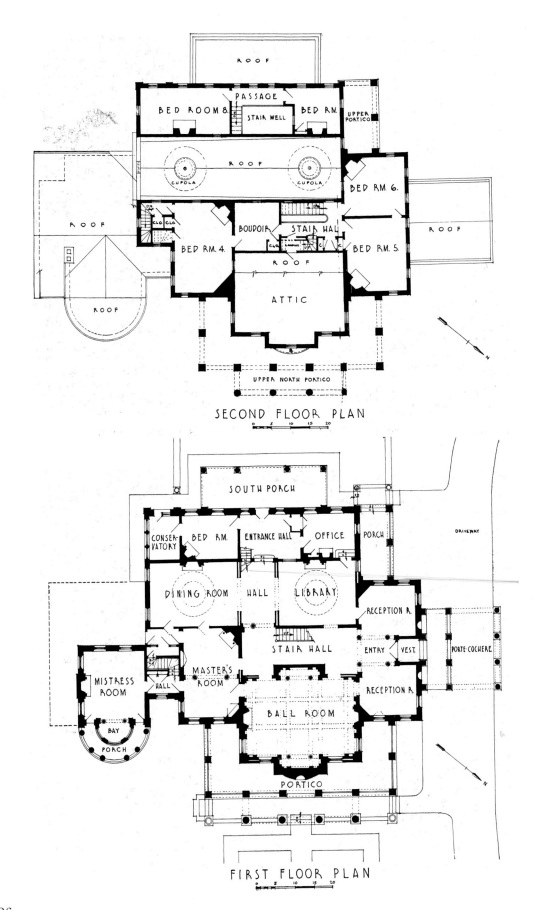

ROOF

PASSAGE

BED ROOM 8. STAIR WELL BED RM. UPPER PORTICO

ROOF

ROOF

CUPOLA CUPOLA

BED RM. 6.

ROOF

DN CLO CLO

BOUDOIR STAIR HALL

ROOF

BED RM. 4. CLO CV CV BED RM. 5.

ROOF

ROOF

ATTIC

ROOF

UPPER NORTH PORTICO

N

SECOND FLOOR PLAN

0 5 10 15 20

SOUTH PORCH

DRIVEWAY

CONSER-VATORY BED RM. ENTRANCE HALL OFFICE PORCH

DINING ROOM HALL LIBRARY

RECEPTION R.

PORTE-COCHERE

STAIR HALL ENTRY VEST

MISTRESS ROOM HALL MASTER'S ROOM

RECEPTION R.

BAY

PORCH

BALL ROOM

N

PORTICO

FIRST FLOOR PLAN

0 5 10 15 20

MAGNOLIA GROVE, Greensboro, Alabama

Magnolia Grove, the ante-bellum ancestral home of Richmond Pearson Hobson, is one of Alabama's three state shrines, and one of its finest Neo-Classic mansions. Situated in an extraordinarily beautiful grove of giant magnolia trees at the head of Main Street in Greensboro, the house enjoys one of the finest landscaping achievements in the state. The expansive formal garden covering acres of intricate boxwood patterns was once a garden show place, and even today in its reduced proportions, it is still filled with the century-old fragrance of choice boxwood.

Built in 1835 by Colonel Isaac Croom, Magnolia Grove was erected on the most inspiring hillrise of the Colonel's entire quarter section plantation. In time, other fine homes took shape in the vicinity, but the Croom home stand today, the resplendent queen of all those about her.

Colonel Croom arrived in the Black Belt in the late twenties with his new bride, Sarah Pearson Croom, sister of North Carolina's Chief Justice Richmond Pearson. Justice Pearson's son and namesake served as ambassador to Italy and minister to both Greece and Persia. Both of these renowned gentlemen made visits with their kinsmen at Magnolia Grove.

The master of the grove became a man of esteem and influence in the new state, and too, he became very wealthy from his large slave-holdings and his thousands of acres of cotton producing land. A devout Episcopalian, he was one of the five founders of The University of the South at Sewanee, having given $100,000.00 toward the foundation fund.

The Crooms left no heirs, so upon their passing, Magnolia Grove became the property of Sarah Croom Pearson, daughter of Chief Justice Pearson. Her mother was Margaret Williams, whose grandfather, Joseph Williams, because he owned all of Surrey County, Virginia, was known as the Duke of Surrey. He was so fabulously rich that he equipped an entire regiment of troops during the Revolutionary War.

The new mistress of the plantation was married to Judge James M. Hobson, also of North Carolina. His mother, Anne Morehead, was a sister to Governor Morehead of that state. Hobson served twenty years as probate judge of Hale County, and in 1898 was appointed by President William McKinley as postmaster of Greensboro.

To this union were born four sons and three daughters. Margaret Williams and Sarah Anne, both writers of novels and books of poetry, live today at Magnolia Grove with their brother Joseph Hobson, scholar of the classics and professor of high repute. One of Sarah Anne's books, "In Old Alabama," is filled with charming tales about life in the pioneer days of the state. A third daughter, Mrs. Florence Morrison of Hammond, Louisiana, also won laurels as a poetess. Colonel James M. Hobson graduated from West Point and returned to become a professor there. The eldest son, Samuel Augustus Hobson, led an illustrious life in Haleyville, Alabama.

While all of the Hobson children made their own distinctive marks in life, it remained for Richmond Pearson Hobson to achieve international renown. As a child, Richmond Pearson Hobson, like the other children of neighboring plantations, grew up amid good times and much gaiety. But his fun was tempered by strict governesses who taught him the art of studious concentration. And theirs was a job well done, for at the youthful age of fourteen, Richmond Pearson entered the Naval Academy at Annapolis. His brilliance of mind was attested by the fact that four years later, he graduated at the top of his class, the first southern boy to achieve such scholastic honors. Young Hobson then journeyed to France and studied at the *Ecole Nationale Superieure des Mines* and the *Ecole d'Application du Genie Maritime* in Paris, where he was the first American, as well as the first person born outside French soil, to win the highest scholastic awards from these schools.

It was a few years later, on the night of June 3, 1898, in Santiago Harbor when the Spanish-American War was raging, that Richmond Pearson Hobson became overnight the hero of the nation. Braving the guns of Morro Castle, a series of planted mines, and the broadside batteries along the narrow channel entrance to Santiago Bay, Hobson led seven men on an escapade said to be one of the most brilliant deeds of heroism in the entire military history of the nation. Facing withering cannon fire and certain death, Hobson and his men sunk a dismantled coal barge, the *Merrimac,* in the narrow channel and bottled up the Spanish fleet. After clinging all night to floating rafts, Hobson was rescued by the Spanish Admiral Cervera who so admired the daring feat that he sent his chief-of-staff under a flag of truce to Hobson's superior officer with a flattering letter extolling the heroism and bravery of Hobson. For this bravery, in 1933 he was presented the nation's highest military award, the Congressional Medal of Honor, by Franklin D. Roosevelt. A year later he was retired from the U.S. Navy with the rank of Rear Admiral. It is interesting to note that as a student of naval history, Hobson many years ago warned against an attack by the Japanese such as occurred at Pearl Harbor.

Upon his return to the United States after the Santiago exploit, the handsome hero of the *Merrimac* was besieged by admiring ladies and he soon established a cross-country kissing reputation which earned for him the label, "The hero of the merry smack!"

A brilliant naval career in the Philippines followed, and then for more than a decade Hobson made a outstanding record as a congressman in Washington, where he championed a strong navy and national prohibition. Upon leaving politics, Hobson settled down to writing and lecturing. His books include "Buck Jones at Annapolis," "The Sinking of the Merrimac," "Why America Should Hold Naval Supremacy," "Fortification of the Panama Canal," and "Alcohol, the Great Destroyer."

But always the hero of the Merrimac found time to return frequently to Magnolia Grove, the childhood home where he had spent so many happy days fishing, riding, swimming, and growing up. It was to Magnolia Grove that he brought his vast array of treasures collected during his years of travel. The two large rooms preserve the many medals, the rare books and historic relics which he gathered. Most noted of all is the nameplate taken from the *Merrimac,* a piece so valued that museums all over the world have tried to obtain it.

Recognizing the great service that Hobson performed not only for Alabama, but for the entire nation, the Alabama legislature in 1943 voted a $7,000.00 restoration fund to Magnolia Grove, along with an annual maintenance stipend. Then on May 1, 1947, Magnolia Grove was dedicated as a state shrine.

Magnolia Grove bears evidence of other wars and other battles. Displayed alongside his father's trophies is a British Military Medal presented to Master Sergeant G. H. Hobson by British General H. R. Alexander for daring exploits performed during the early days of the North African campaign of World War II. The award was approved by His Majesty, King George VI of England, November 24, 1944.

Magnolia Grove, with its six massive Doric columns, is one of Alabama's finest examples of the Greek Revival. The house is constructed of handmade brick, seasoned by aging until today they bear clayish colors of variegated texture, flecked by bits of charcoal. The entire façade, including the unadorned pediment, is plastered and painted a gleaming white. The tall Georgian windows of the two front room parlors open as doors onto the picturesque veranda. The veranda at the back of the house also rises two stories, but unlike the bold columns at the front, it is supported by small fluted iron pillars. Just behind the house is the two-story brick apartment with four moderately sized columns patterned in keeping with the large ones of the mother house. It was here that the nine house servants were quartered upstairs, while in the basement kitchen they did the cooking for Colonel Croom and his descendants. But times have changed. A modern kitchen is now a part of the mansion, and the servants' quarters are devoid of the bustling noises and delicious aromas which once prevailed there.

The interior of Magnolia Grove follows the traditional mansion plan, a rectangular shape with central hall dividing large rooms on either side. A distinctive winding staircase with mahogany steps and railing rises from the rear of the broad hall. A bronze chandelier hangs from an unusually beautiful plaster medallion in the center of the hall. The cornice of the wall is finished in the motif of the Egyptian lotus.

Magnolia Grove is little changed from its original status. The love-seats, the family silver, the marble-top tables—they're all there in place. "This is not just a shrine—it is a home, simple in antiques but rich in memories," Miss Margaret Hobson, the present hostess, tells the many visitors who come every year to see the birthplace and shrine of the great Hobson.

Nowhere in the mansion do the rich memories suggest themselves as strongly as when one stops to view the collection of family portraits. Master Croom himself holds forth above the rosewood spinet piano in the parlor, while over the mantel hangs a cheerful portrait of Justice Pearson. Other paintings bring to light the faces of Joseph Williams, the Duke of Surrey; Justice Pearson's mother, Eliza; Sarah Pearson Hobson; Judge James Hobson; Anne Morehead Hobson; kinsman General James White, founder of the City of Knoxville, Tennessee; and others. The latest addition to these portraits is one of Richmond Pearson Hobson dressed in the uniform of Rear Admiral, USN. Painted by Maltby Sykes, the portrait was unveiled the day Magnolia Grove became a state shrine.

Magnolia Grove, one of the finest Greek Revival mansions in Alabama, is a state shrine dedicated to Richmond Pearson Hobson, the hero of the *Merrimac*. It is open daily to the public.

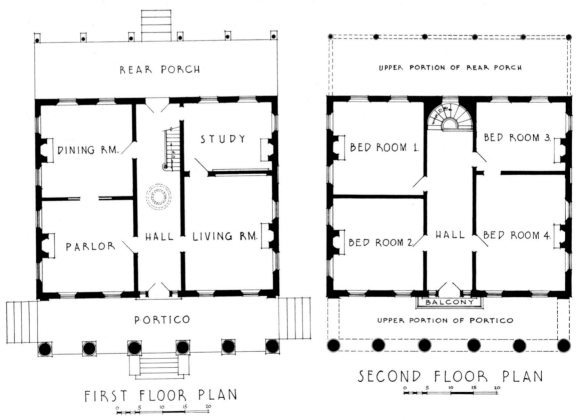

The parlor of Magnolia Grove contains a collection of early family portraits. Over the mantel is seen a century old painting of Richmond Pearson, Chief Justice of North Carolina's Supreme Court.

ISRAEL PICKENS HOME, Greensboro, Alabama

Israel Pickens left an imprint on the destiny of Alabama perhaps greater than any man who ever lived within the state. He was a man of monumental character and achievement, all attained within a short life of forty-seven years.

Pickens led a full and colorful life. He served in the North Carolina legislature, then went to Congress from that state for three terms and declined to run again when he decided to join the trek westward. He was appointed Register of the Land Office in the territorial capital at St. Stephens, in 1817.

It will be recalled that William Wyatt Bibb died shortly after becoming Alabama's first governor, and that his brother, Thomas Bibb, by virtue of his being president of the Alabama senate, served out his brother's unexpired term as acting governor. Thus it was left for Israel Pickens, the second elected governor, to set the broad pattern of creating a state government. Under his direction the capitol was constructed at Cahaba; the judicial courts were established; many new counties were created; a program for building roads and ferries was promoted. During his two terms as governor, he created an effective political machine which overthrew Bibb's supporting Georgia faction and controlled Alabama politics for twenty years.

Pickens was the first chairman of the board of trustees of the newly founded University of Alabama; first president of the Alabama Bible Society; one of the founders of Masonry in Alabama. He entertained LaFayette when he visited Alabama in the spring of 1825. And being keenly interested in mathematics and astronomy, he invented a lunar dial which told the time of night by moonlight.

Being well informed on land possibilities in Alabama, Pickens purchased a large plantation three miles from Greensboro and promoted a highly diversified crop program. He even seeded pasturelands for grazing, a thing unheard of at the time in the Alabama wilderness. He named the plantation Greenwood.

It was in 1821 that Pickens built his mansion. It was furnished luxuriously with an abundance of silver, linens, laces, and with room after room of elegant mahogany suites of furniture. The architecture of the house is similar to that used in perhaps twenty other mansions throughout the state. However, it was one of the very first of its type to be built. The portico of the Banks Home in nearby Eutaw is almost identical with the Pickens Home. While not overly elaborate, the house has good lines and well planned dimensions.

Pickens' background in the national capital, his close associations with the leaders of the country, and his excellent educational training, brought to his new mansion an air of intellectual stimulation and a vibrant way of life.

After leaving the governor's office, Pickens again returned to political service in Washington to fill out the unexpired term of United States Senator Henry Chambers. However, his time there was to be brief. Several months later he became seriously ill and journeyed to Cuba in the hopes of regaining his health, but died in Matanzas, in 1827. The sum of five hundred dollars was appropriated by the Alabama legislature to return his remains to his plantation home in Alabama. Then in 1933 he was removed to the cemetery in Greensboro and appropriate markers erected at the burial site.

The furnishings of the mansion were sold at auction soon after Pickens' death, and a few years later the mansion was dismantled and removed to Greensboro, just down Main Street from Magnolia Grove, the state shrine that honors Richmond Pearson Hobson.

In later years it was owned by the builder's great nephew, William C. Pickens. From him it passed into the hands of Mr. and Mrs. J. F. Brown.

Israel Pickens Home. Built by one of Alabama's great governors as the center of his vast plantation near Greensboro, this place, named Greenwood, was dismantled after the builder's death and erected as a town house on Greensboro's fashionable Main Street. It was built in 1821.

CARLISLE HALL, near Marion, Alabama

Carlisle Hall was built by Edwin Kenworthy Carlisle and originally named Kenworthy Hall. Started in 1827, it required about ten years to build. It is located a mile west of Marion.

The house has eighteen rooms, twelve marble mantels, three staircases—one a tightly designed oblong spiral which ascends three floors—and exceptional plaster cornices and medallions. The timber in the doors, the wainscoting, the windows and the great staircase which rises in the center of the main hall and divides into double stairs on the half-way landing, is the finest oak woodwork found this early in the state. Much of it is treated with false graining.

The brick and stone trim of Carlisle Hall are almost a miracle to behold. The brick mortar, recently analyzed as German cement, is as tightly imbedded as the day it was applied. The brick themselves show no signs of weathered deterioration, nor does the extensive trim of pinkish sandstone, said to be English fieldstone. It is reported that the brick and the sandstone were imported from Europe, as were the twelve marble mantels. This is very probable, due to the fact that ships brought over loads of brick as ballast (Montgomery and Mobile have many streets paved with European brick,) and also the soil around Marion does not lend itself to brick making, consequently wooden houses predominate. The fieldstone has a tiny ribbing effect upon every piece, with about eight ribs to the inch. The brick foundation wall measures forty-two inches, and the walls throughout the house are twenty-eight inches in thickness.

Carlisle Hall is a highly individual house; there is no other even similar in design in Alabama. Disregarding the popularity of the Greek Revival, its builder used a variety of styles, especially the Romanesque arch used so profusely over all windows and doors. Then the balcony rail suggests a Moorish derivation, while the balcony's overhanging copper roof follows Japanese temple lines. The front porch is a recent and rather crude replacement of what once must have been quite a handsome one. This porch is the only part of the house not original.

Carlisle Hall has many features of special interest to architects. It is unfortunate that the architect is unknown, because he must have been a person of unusual skill. It has been reported by some that Benjamin Henry Latrobe, architect of the United States Capitol, designed Carlisle Hall. Such a claim appears to be totally unfounded, since Latrobe died in 1820, seven years before Carlisle Hall was started.

134

Carlisle Hall. Alabama has only one outstanding early Gothic house, and it is fine that the one example proved to be so well designed and built of such splendid material as to attract widespread attention.

Romanesque windows and doorheads of pink sandstone, superlative brick masonry, twelve marble mantels, a copper roof, and three unique staircases, make Carlisle Hall, near Marion, a distinctive architectural achievement.

The staircase at Carlisle Hall has fine balusters and newel posts. The backside of the stairs is paneled with oak.

135

PORTER KING HOME, Marion, Alabama

Mammoth camellia bushes more than a century old all but hide from view Marion's finest mansion, built in 1849 by Captain Porter King. While grand in scope, the house is noted for its simplicity which is keynoted in the tall, slender columns, similar to those used in Mobile's Bragg Home.

Captain King organized and commanded a Confederate company known as the Marion Rifles. During one of the major battles at Manassas, Captain King was standing beside General Barnard E. Bee, who, upon watching General Thomas J. Jackson and his forces withstand a withering enemy attack, exclaimed, "Look at Jackson, standing like a stonewall!"—thereby giving Jackson his widely known nickname of Stonewall.

The King estate was sold to Dr. William Barron in 1906 and later passed to his daughter, Mrs. Joseph W. Arburthnot, Senior, who occupies it with her family today.

HANNA-WEISSINGER HOME, Marion, Alabama

The Hanna-Weissinger Home in Marion has an appearance which immediately brings to mind the White House of the Confederacy in Richmond. Rather ambitiously conceived, expertly built and graciously maintained, the mansion is one of the most charming in the entire Black Belt. It was built long before the Civil War by Harry Hurt. It passed to his daughter, Nellie, who, with her husband, Dr. R. C. Hanna, lived in it for many years.

It is now owned by Dr. William Weissinger.

Note the expertly carpentered side entrance and the beaded cornice trim above the columns, both of which add immeasurably to the charm of the house.

PITTS' FOLLY, Uniontown, Alabama

Pitts' Folly in Uniontown is one of the Black Belt's most ambitious mansions. No less than a dozen tales are recorded as to how it got its name, all of them centering around the absurdity that Phillip Henry Pitts was building such a huge mansion that it was indeed a folly.

However, Pitts was a man of strong conviction, and was not to be moved by the disparaging remarks of his less ambitious townsmen. He was a man of unusual learning and kept voluminous diaries, five of which are now in the possession of Davidson College in North Carolina. In one of these he recorded, "On Friday, February 27, 1852, I commenced raising my new house in Uniontown," thus establishing the exact date of Pitts' Folly's beginning. Later, the diary says that it was finished and moved into in April, 1853.

Shortly after building his house, his total assets, listed in his diary for tax purposes, were fixed at $170,000.00, an accumulation which indeed rated him as a man of means.

Pitts married Margaret Davidson, daughter of Uniontown's Colonel A. C. Davidson, whose family founded Davidson College. Pitts himself was a heavy donor to the college during his life time.

B. F. Parsons of Marion, who also was architect of the Perry County courthouse in Marion, drew the details and plans for Pitts' Folly. A slave named Reuben Green made all the lathes used in the construction work.

The mansion has fourteen Doric columns, nine across the front and five to the left side as one looks to the front. When the mansion was restored in 1948, these old columns were allowed to retain their weathered look. The columns are very closely spaced, with almost a rhythmical touch of beauty. Two solid walnut Doric columns grace the recessed front entrance.

The house is built in the traditional square shape with a central hall dividing it. One of the clever features found here is a secret staircase, built into the wall and not visible from any exterior point.

Pitts' Folly has remained in the Pitts family and is today owned by Mrs. Harry N. Pharr, a direct descendant of the builder.

Pitts' Folly turned out not the folly that Uniontown people predicted, but one of the Black Belt's most ambitious mansions.

WATTS-PARKMAN-GILLMAN HOME, Selma, Alabama

The dying of Cahaba, the early state capital, had much to do with the upbuilding of Selma and the springing to life of its many ante-bellum mansions, none of which are quite as grand as the home built in 1853 by Colonel Edward Watts.

The Watts Mansion, now commonly referred to as the Gillman Home, is built in much the same manner as several Natchez mansions, with a striking similarity in parts to historic Stanton Hall. Colonel Watts, being a man of classical background and abundant means, wanted the finest mansion in all the region. So he hired a professional architect, Thomas Helm Lee, a cousin of General Robert E. Lee, to translate his own envisioned splendor into an architectural delight.

Located on the corner of Mabry and McLeod Streets in downtown Selma, the mansion grounds cover nearly a city block. Architect Lee fashioned as stately a portico as one would hope to view. While he applied the Corinthian order, he held it to severe restraint, using only a single band of acanthus leaves around the lower extremities of the column capitals fashioned from cast iron. Six equally spaced, thirty-foot fluted columns flank the highly picturesque portico. The solemnity of arrangement is given an exquisite, femininelike touch by the addition of a lacy grille balcony running the sixty-foot length of the porch. A second entrance at the left side of the house features a single story porch with iron-grille trellises, designed with grape clusters and leaves, serving as posts.

The biggest surprise of the Watts Home is the rear façade. For here we find a veranda with two lofty Doric columns, and an upstairs porch guarded by a richly ivy patterned iron-grille railing, crested with small *fleur-de-lis*. The veranda, unlike the one at the front, does not run the full breadth of the house, but is bound at either end by a small room on both the first and second floors. An outside staircase winds up from the first floor veranda to the porch above.

The original kitchen with great Dutch ovens is in the backyard and still intact, though not used as such today. The dainty cupola does not exemplify the Greek elegance of all the other exterior details.

Inside, the Watts Home shows the same qualities of rich design as are seen from every compass point on the outside. Upstairs and down, a T-shaped hall divides the arrangement of rooms. A central hall runs the full length of the mid-section, then the left side is cut into half by still another hall. The great twenty-by-thirty-foot drawing room on the first floor is formed by this division of halls. It is the finest room in the mansion. The plaster work, with large rosettes widely spaced at the bottom of the cornice, and tiny ones closely formed at the top, is excellent in both design and workmanship. One grand metal piece serves as the cornice for the stately pier mirror and the floor-length windows at the front. The same pattern is carried out on the metal cornices of the side windows and the mirror overhanging the richly carved mantel of

140

gleaming white Carrara marble.

Across the hall at the front, the parlor is separated from the dining hall by a broad opening with a free standing Corinthian column on either side. The capitals of the columns are painted gold, and the parlor is referred to as the Gold Room. The French parlor furniture has gold thread running through the tapestry weave.

The staircase flanks, not the central hall, but the abbreviated one at the backside of the drawing room. It is a straight-run stairway, and the walls along it are decorated with hand-painted imitation panels, highly suggestive of real ones. These hand-painted plaster walls have been there for some eighty years and still retain unusual qualities of the original color.

But Colonel Watts would not be bested: he was determined to have a spiral staircase, so much the vogue of the time. He had one built to connect the second floor with the cupola. The spindles of the stair railing are in natural finish of what appears to be walnut. This staircase is highly ingenious in that it is constructed around a central core post which extends the entire height of the stairwell, and around it the treads wind and wind and wind, finally reaching the observation point of the cupola. In sheer finesse of artistry, this staircase is second only to the cornice trim of the drawing room.

But Colonel Watts was not for long to enjoy the beauties which he had had created in his majestic mansion. In 1864, only eleven years after the house was built, the lure of Texas beckoned, and he packed up, sold out and took his family westward to broader plains, yet in all probability, not to a finer mansion.

The house was purchased by John S. Parkman, a Selma banker, and he too was slated for short residence in the mansion. In 1870 his banking establishment became entangled with Reconstruction authorities and he was thrown into the Federal prison at Cahaba.

His Selma friends devised an almost Wild West escape for him. They hired a river boat, dressed themselves in Mardi Gras, masquerade fashion, and set out for Cahaba, only a few miles down the Alabama River. Upon arrival there, they marched up Capital Street, singing and frolicking in ribald jestry, making noises with gourds, horns and loudish instruments. So rollicking was their hilarity that the Reconstruction military troops, including the prison guards, were distracted and came out to view the parade. And during their moment of laxity, Parkman escaped from old Fort Morgan and dived into the Alabama River. Legend has it that he was never seen or heard of afterwards.

That same year the house and property was sold at auction. Emile Gillman paid $12,500.00 for the entire estate. He lived there for many years, and then the mansion passed to his daughter, Augusta Gillman Bibb, the present occupant.

The Watts-Parkman-Gillman Home remains Selma's finest house, as well as a rich contribution to the high order of Greek Revival architecture attained in Alabama. Its beauties, richly conceived, are as enduring as the splendor of the Athenian temples of the Old World—enduring in that they never become out-moded, old fashioned.

The Watts-Parkman-Gillman Home, designed by an architect-cousin of General Robert E. Lee, is the finest of Selma's many ante-bellum mansions. It contains a superlative wedding of the ornamental iron trim with the Greek Revival colonnades.

The Watts-Parkman-Gillman Home. The side entrance is an excellent example of ornamental iron used to its fullest advantage.

The rear portico, graced with columns and iron-lace, follows the general plan used in numerous of the finer Natchez mansions. The kitchen is the dependency to the right.

143

THE WELCH HOME, Selma, Alabama

The Welch Home in Selma is one of those few ante-bellum homes which has always remained immaculate and never been allowed to suffer neglect. For eighty-odd years now the Welch's have cared for this lovely old mansion. Inside and out, it has always been freshly clean and well preserved since that day in 1887 when William Pressley Welch bought the home, covering almost a city block, from George Cater for the sum of $5,000.00. When he informed his wife of the purchase he had made, Mrs. Welch exclaimed, "There are too many porches and too many halls to sweep!" But her regrets were shortlived, for the Welch's lived a full life and reared nine children in the home, two of whom, Misses Bessie and Kate Welch, still live there.

The Welch Home was built in 1858 for William B. King. Shortly afterwards it was sold to a Confederate Major named Siddons, who in turn sold it to George Cater. The floor plan is of equal proportions on both floors and quite simple: rectangular in shape with a forty-two foot hall dividing two rooms on either side. On the ground floor there are twin parlors to the left—one for the grown-ups and one for the children, and the Welch's always followed a strict rule of entertaining visitors in the parlor befitting their age. Across the hall are the dining room and the master's bedroom, to the rear. Upstairs there are four bedrooms and two baths, the latter being modern innovations made from original dressing rooms.

There is much of the original furniture remaining in the home, and the numerous rosewood trimmed chairs and settees are especially fine, as are several of the bedroom suites and baby beds.

The finest architectural achievement in the Welch Home is the stately staircase, unsupported and extending in a straight line twenty-four feet to the second floor. But it does not end there. The banister swerves about face and runs half way down the upstairs hall and there it begins another exquisite climb to the attic rooms. As one stands at the bottom of the stairs and peers up at the forty-seven foot ascent, the view is one of outstanding harmony in design and proportions. Most ante-bellum mansions have a less pretentious stairway leading to the attic, and it is unusual to find such an excellent execution of stairs as this, which greatly adds to the over-all interior arrangement. Still another stairway, used by servants to carry up wood for fires and water for bathing, leads up from a side portico.

The ground floor hall has identical doorways at either end, the motif being paneled sidelights and rectangular transoms. The design is bold and simple. All of the door and window casings throughout the house are simple yet strong in design, and most befitting the general plan. The mantels are wooden and plain. The floors, with the exception of the dining room, are of the original heart pine planks. An inlaid oak floor was added to the dining room when such was the fashion about a quarter of a century ago.

The chandeliers in the downstairs rooms are bronze with cherubs, having been imported from France. The wooden molding around the ceiling cornice of the parlors and dining room is made of thin layers of wooden trim, graduated in a shelving effect.

Houses have a way of taking on the qualities of their owners, and as such, the Welch Home reflects a spirit of hospitality and Christianity. Since first coming to Alabama from Virginia in the late 1830's, the Welch family have been leaders in the Baptist Church. The Welch Home, for years without end, has been open to Baptist ministers and as a result it has often been called "The White House for Baptist Preachers." Ministers knew that hospitality always awaited them at the Welch Home and often they came at three or four o'clock in the morning and rested a few days before continuing their journey.

Recently when the Selma Baptist Church celebrated its one-hundredth anniversary, a pair of silver vases was presented Miss Kate Welch, honoring her as the living member who had rendered the most faithful service to the work of the church.

Even though William Pressley Welch lived to be seventy-nine, he undoubtedly would have enjoyed many more healthy years at his big white house, had it not been for an ill twist of fate. One day when Master Welch was on his way fishing, a downtown store sign fell on his head, killing him instantly.

Welch Home. Due to its abounding hospitality for ministers, the Welch Home came to be known as The White House for Baptist Ministers.

KENAN PLACE, near Selma, Alabama

Kenan Place is four miles from Selma on the old Summerfield pike. Built in 1826 by Dr. Algernon Jefferies, it has a quaintness of design all its own.

The stately façade, forming the central body of the house, is purely classic, while the wings added to either side—wings which might well have been outdoor kitchens or slave quarter dependencies—keynote a Federal, or early American, influence, all of which makes for a distinctively interesting portico. A more classic example of wing additions is found at Oak Lawn, near Huntsville.

A small hall running the length of the porch has a miniaturelike staircase that swerves brokenly upward. The parlor is in the left front wing; the dining hall in the right wing, and the large living room, with the original unjointed floor of varying widths, is in the center of the house directly behind the hall.

The present owners, Dr. and Mrs. James Kenan, take great pride in showing the many visitors the scar left upon the house by the Civil War. They roll back a corner of the rug and display the jagged black ring burnt into the parlor floor by soldiers of Yankee General James Wilson who set fire to a pile of furniture and left it ablaze. A vigilant slave dashed in when they had gone and extinguished the fire. This is one place where no myth has grown out of hand-me-down tales: proof is plentiful. The plantation charm of Kenan Place is greatly enhanced by the landscaping of giant camellias, boxwood, and roses.

Dr. Jefferies sold the plantation to Mrs. Betty Douglas, who soon afterwards sold it to Judge Ezekiel Pickens, a Dallas County lawyer and judge, said to have used the then popular "science" of phrenology in sizing up defendants for judgment.

The plantation has been known as Kenan Place since 1854 when it was purchased by Colonel Thomas Kenan who served as a pallbearer in Selma at the funeral of William Rufus King, Alabama's only Vice President of the United States.

Kenan Place, with wings of strong Federal influence, still has the charred ring on the parlor floor left when Wilson's Raiders set fire to the house, only to have it extinguished by a vigilant slave.

CHAPTER V

Montgomery and Central Alabama Region

Montgomery

Lowndesboro

Greenville

Pleasant Hill

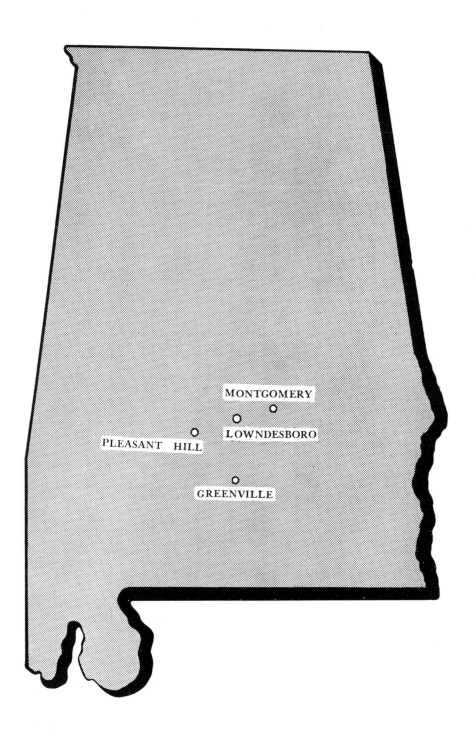

(Montgomery and Central Alabama Region)

TENNENT LOMAX HOME, Montgomery, Alabama

Built on lot number one of New Philadelphia, part of the old settlement from which the city of Montgomery grew, the Tennent Lomax House embodies the finest of Greek Revival line and form. It was built in 1847-48 by James J. Gilmer, brother of George R. Gilmer, governor of Georgia, but it had hardly been completed when it was purchased, February 13, 1849, by Reuben C. Shorter, Jr., brother of John G. Shorter, governor of Alabama. Mrs. Shorter, after her husband's death, married Captain Tennent Lomax on March 25, 1857. A man of brilliance, culture and means, Lomax left with his regiment for the battlefields of Virginia when the Civil War started. But his military service was shortlived. He fell mortally wounded, June 1, 1862, during the battle of Seven Pines. His beautiful widow never again married and lived in the fashionable mansion until her death, June 30, 1907. The home is today headquarters for an insurance company.

The heavy flourishing and boldness of the plaster medallions and cornice work of the parlors and hall lean heavily toward the Roman influence, instead of the more refined Greek touches.

Tennent Lomax Home. Here is fenestration at its very best. The rear of this side view is a later addition, however it was constructed in copious detail after the parent body of the house. The pilastered doorway with its dentiled cornice adds classical quality to the broad length of the siding.

Done in excellent workmanship, the spiral staircase extends its unbroken length from the first to the second and on to the third floor of the mansion.

Tennent Lomax Home. The ornamental iron balcony was once a favorite sitting spot at the Lomax House when ladies and gentlemen rode in fine carriages along fashionable Court Street. Montgomery became the state capital in 1846 and statesmen, rich planters and politicians came in great numbers and frequency to transact business and legislate new laws in the fast growing city.

DICKERSON-ARNOLD-GREIL HOME, Montgomery, Alabama

Montgomery has had more of its ante-bellum mansions razed than any other city in Alabama. Literally by the dozens they have been torn down to make way for new homes, new apartments, and modern business establishments.

The Dickerson-Arnold-Greil Home, like many of the others, has been taken over for business purposes and today serves as offices for the city education department. It was built on a tract of land which Andrew Dexter purchased from the federal government, August 13, 1817, the lots being part of the area known as New Philadelphia. From Dexter the land passed through several hands, including John Falconer, John Goldthwaite, and Benjamin D. Hassell, before John P. Figh sold it to John P. Dickerson, September 29, 1854, for $1,000.00, whereupon Dickerson soon afterwards began construction of his mansion.

Being one of the city's finest new mansions, it was occupied by Governor John G. Shorter during his tenure of office from 1861-62. However, he did not own the house.

David S. Arnold bought the estate, January 24, 1865, for $60,500.00. Then after a series of squabbles over mortgages, it was bought at public auction, February 5, 1878, by Mrs. Mena Greil. She and her family held it until 1920 when it became the University Club, a short-lived experiment.

The exterior of the house is a blend of the Greek and Roman influences. The columns and the entablature are styled largely after the Parthenon, and the windowheads have Greek trim of dogtooth dentils. Supporting the lintels of the windows, as well as the doors, are abbreviated consoles covered with acanthus leaves. Featuring this same console styling are the four brackets supporting the iron balcony, only each console is divided into two large scrolls instead of one.

The dining room is the finest thing in the mansion. It has the finest paneling of any room in Alabama. The solid mahogany panels rise six feet from the floor. Then a series of inset plaster panels painted white are fitted between the eighteen mahogany pilasters distributed rhythmically around the four walls. These in turn are crowned with a really grand mahogany cornice, broad in width and of exquisite Greek detail. The mantelpiece, though, with simple lines and bearing a note of restraint, is the *pièce de resistance* of the room. Three large slabs of white marble form the basis of the mantel. A two-inch strip of brass, cast with the Greek fret used throughout the room, protects the inner dimensions of the marble from heat. Then, to add further elegance to the room, the architect, with a display of brilliance, erected a superbly fluted and free-standing mahogany column on either side of the mantel. And as a wainscot cap for the entire lower paneling, there was added a classic mahogany strip of Greek fret eight inches in width.

The exquisiteness of design and the unadulterated purity of Greek elegance in the room is closely akin to the Greek perfection achieved in the old Knox Home, now razed, which was the finest Greek edifice ever built in Montgomery.

154

The dining hall, with eighteen mahogany pilasters and two free-standing columns which John P. Dickerson built into his mansion, has the finest mahogany paneling of any room in the state.

The Dickerson-Arnold-Greil Home was known as the governor's mansion while occupied by Governor John G. Shorter from 1861-62.

TEAGUE HOME, Montgomery, Alabama

The Teague Home has been an arbiter of architectural fashion in Alabama's capital city since it was constructed by Berry Owens in 1848. Owens, who operated livery stables, sold his business and his new mansion and left Montgomery, October 1, 1852. It was then held by three different owners before it was purchased, March 28, 1889, by William Martin Teague, one time mayor of Montgomery. The Teague family has since held continuous proprietorship.

When General James Wilson entered Montgomery, April 12, 1865, for a week's stay before moving on to Tuskegee, he used the old Governor Thomas Hill Watts House, now the chapel of Saint Margaret's Hospital, as his official headquarters, but on several occasions he visited the Teague Home, then occupied by Federal troops, and from its porch he read the proclamation which declared Montgomery to be under Federal occupation.

While the exterior is fashioned with very excellent Ionic stone columns, the interior has some examples of beautifully fluted, free standing Corinthian columns, and a staircase that starts its climb in a straight-run manner for fourteen steps and then swerves off-center into a spiral formation.

The dependencies of the Teague Home remain intact in the commodious rear courtyard, surrounded by a high brick wall.

In recent years the red brick house has been painted an egg-shellish pink, very much the color seen on the thatch roofed cottages in Devonshire and Cornwall, England.

Teague Home. Ever since it was built in 1848, the Teague Home has been an arbiter of architectural fashion in Alabama's capital city. Its six Ionic columns are magnificently beautiful.

TYSON HOME, Lowndesboro, Alabama

The Archibald Tyson home, built in the mid-1850's, is Lowndesboro's most strikingly individual mansion. It has two major porticoes, one with six Doric columns, the other with four. The symmetry of the pediments is excellent. The house is built in the shape of an L, allowing cross ventilation for every room. A one-story porch extends around both sides of the court at the rear. The house has remained in the Tyson family until this day. The quality of its architecture and the endurance of its wooden construction retain their full appeal, even though time has dealt rather unkindly with the old house.

THOMAS-HAGOOD HOUSE, Lowndesboro, Alabama

Lowndesboro, the name of an Alabama community which holds connotations of patrician splendor during the ante-bellum era, is filled with fine houses, because rich plantation owners built their mansions, their churches along one tree-lined avenue, while their plantation lands extended into all the surrounding region. They desired neighbors instead of remote plantation life. At one time there were approximately thirty of these mansions, but many have since been reduced to ashes. Perhaps the most distinguished of those remaining is the house built in 1853 by an itinerant builder named Nunnley for George Thomas, local squire. Mr. Nunnley built other Lowndesboro mansions, all of which bear certain striking similarities. The portico of this house extends completely around two sides of the structure in a sumptuous manner. The cornice brackets are very elaborate, the larger ones almost bordering onto consoles. The lovely iron-lace balconies, the broad and well lighted entrances, the Italian black marble mantels in the parlors—all lend qualities of good taste and refinement to the house. People in the community still tell about the time the massive crystal chandelier in the hall fell and crashed into shattered fragments. For years the house was owned by Ransom Meadows, the last survivor of Lowndes County's Confederate veterans. It is now in the possession of his daughter, Mrs. R. B. Hagood.

OLD HOMESTEAD, Lowndesboro, Alabama

This Lowndesboro mansion, with its bold columns and broad verandas, very much suggests the dimensions of the man who built it in 1823. Dixon Hall Lewis weighed the tidy sum of five-hundred pounds. Thus it was necessary that he have a great double door for the veranda, extraordinarily large white pillars, rooms of immense proportions, and specially designed furniture in the house, because he wanted the house to depict the man.

A sandstone boulder at the entrance bears the inscription, "Old Homestead—1823," an early date indeed for a mansion of this type to have been built in the locality and a date which about fixes the very beginning of the grand manner mansion building era in central Alabama.

When Dixon Hall Lewis traveled to and from Washington, where he served his district as Congressman, stage coaches had to be equipped with extra heavy springs in order to accommodate his mountainous proportions. And on the floor of Congress, his colleagues often remarked that Alabama had the "largest" representation in Congress.

Old Homestead has an elaborate portico, and the flanking façade, while built of the same massive materials and identical pattern, is limited to smaller confines.

The mansion is now owned by Mr. and Mrs. Crowell A. Pate who have recently restored it throughout.

Old Homestead was built in 1823 by Congressman Dixon Hall Lewis who weighed five-hundred pounds.

The side porch adds an interesting touch to Old Homestead.

DUNKLIN HOME, Greenville, Alabama

Greenville's loveliest ante-bellum mansion was built in 1857 by James Law Dunklin. The architect is said to have been the Englishman who designed the Womack Home on the Ridge, a plantation settlement twelve miles northwest of Greenville. This unusually beautiful home remained directly in the family until sold in 1947 to Dr. James E. Kendrick, who is the cousin of a former owner.

A massive ornamental iron fence surrounds the expansive and beautifully landscaped estate, located at 504 Fort Dale Road.

BELVOIR, Pleasant Hill, Alabama

Pleasant Hill's Belvoir was built in the center of a large plantation by Reuben Saffold, Chief Justice of the Alabama Supreme Court. The date of 1825 is affixed to the crest of the drain pipe, as was so often the custom of the early builders.

Few ante-bellum mansions have known a more glamorous social life in which important personages mingled so frequently with the Saffold family. Judge Saffold was one of the early political leaders of the region who helped shape the destiny of a territory into permanent statehood. He also had a significant role in founding the first courts and establishing a code of law for the new state.

Belvoir is now owned by Mrs. J. M. Mason of Birmingham who uses the Pleasant Hill mansion as a summer home. In many ways the house resembles very closely the Hagood Home in Lowndesboro, the columns and banister trim being identical.

UNDERWOOD-MAYO HOME, Pleasant Hill, Alabama

The Underwood-Mayo Home is one of several plantation mansions in the Pleasant Hill community. While not spectacular, it is an orderly approach to a livable plantation home. The two story portico is a happy balance of the square and round Doric columniation, further enriched by four fluted wall pilasters. Its disciplined pediment, with sunray louvre, gives to the portal an appearance of unity. Most interesting room in the house is the raised dining room built at the end of a rear ell, entered through a breezeway beyond the central hall. The now abandoned brick kitchen, with huge fireplace, was built directly underneath the dining hall, and steaming food brought up a stairway. The house was built in 1845 by Green Underwood and remained in his family until recently when purchased by Mr. and Mrs. John Mayo who have done extensive restoration work.

CHAPTER VI

Mobile Region

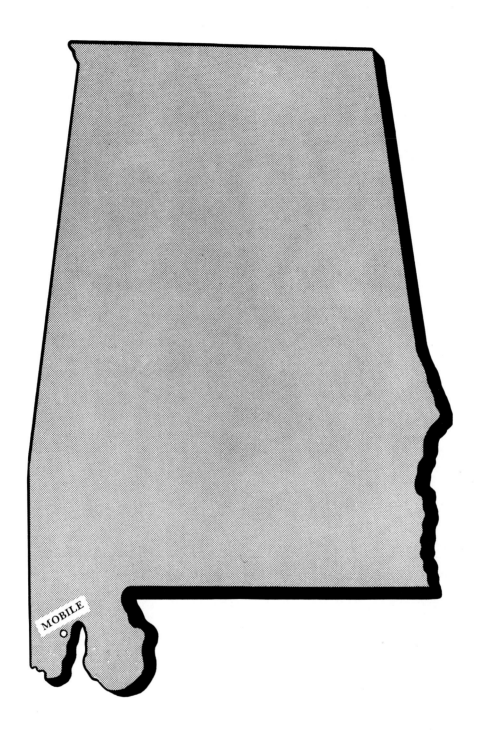

MOBILE

(Mobile Region)

BRAGG HOME, Mobile, Alabama

The Bragg Home on Mobile's Springhill Avenue has a most beautiful setting. The mansion is surrounded by more than sixty acres of grounds, and the great semi-circle driveway is artistically clustered with hundreds of azalea and camellia bushes, not to mention the dozens of liveoak trees grown from acorns planted by Judge John Bragg himself. These trees grew in place of the grove chopped down to give Confederate artillery free range to shell the approaching Federal troops.

The mansion was built on property bought, May 10, 1855, by Judge John Bragg from W. H. Pratt for the sum of $7,500.00. The tract already had a small house on it —to the rear of the present mansion—and was located in the fashionable suburb of Summerville, now part of Mobile.

Judge Bragg, a North Carolinian, came to Mobile in 1835 and started a law practice. In 1842 he was elected circuit judge, a post he held for nine years. In 1852 he was elected to the United States Congress. In the meantime, in 1847 he had married Mary Frances Hall of Lowndesboro, Alabama.

Judge Bragg hired the best architect available when he started his house shortly after returning to Alabama from Congress in 1854. He employed Thomas S. James who has to his credit several Greek Revival structures. No other architect in Mobile left so rich a heritage of classic beauty. More than any other single person, he brought the Greek Revival motif into a city almost completely dominated by French influence of wrought iron, compact dwellings and on-the-sidewalk structures. He brought the white pillars and the spacious concept of living.

The Bragg Home is Thomas S. James's most beautiful residence, and Mobile's most handsome Greek Revival mansion. Built as it was in the mid 1850's, it shows a decided about-face from the massive columns, temple-like pediments, in that James designed tall, spindly columns which must be considered as Doric, since they fit the broad confines of no other order. And he placed them densely about the three-sided veranda. Another innovation was placing the front entrance, not in the center of the portico, but slightly to the right side where it opens into the hall with spiral staircase. This arrangement allowed for an enormous parlor which extends approximately fifty feet in length —the center being broken by two free-standing columns which support three broad arches. These columns are identical with those used on the portico.

The house has fourteen rooms, seven of them bedrooms which measure up to twenty-three feet in each direction. Each bedroom has a marble mantel. The ceilings of the parlor are sixteen feet high.

The only ornamental iron employed in the structure is in the façade balcony, which hangs, not over the door, but dead-center of the portico and over a floor length window.

The T-shape plan is used for the general parti. This is the plan employed frequently in the Greek Revival mansions of the South, and wisely so, because it allows for much fuller ventilation. The idea is to give bedrooms the vantage spots of the back corners, allowing for ventilation on three sides. This T-shape plan is found at Rosemount and the Varner-Alexander Home in Tuskegee.

Fate dealt the Bragg Home an unkindly, tragic hand during the Civil War. Judge Bragg, fearing for the safety of his elegant new furnishings, removed them from the town mansion and carted them up river to his home at Indiantown Bluff, thinking that the remoteness of the spot would surely make for safety. But it was upon Indiantown Bluff that Wilson's Raiders pounced, burning Judge Bragg's house and all the furnishings stored within. The furniture included some of the most handsome and expensive ever brought to Mobile. It is said that the parlor carpets were of "white velvet embossed in pink flowers," and that the parlor suite was of carved rosewood upholstered in satin damask. All of these furnishings had been selected in New York, Philadelphia and Baltimore.

It has often been reported that this is the General Braxton Bragg Home. Such is not the case. General Bragg did live on the estate for a short time while building jetties at the mouth of Mobile Bay during the Civil War, but he lived in the small house at the rear.

The mansion has passed through several ownerships since Judge Bragg died. For a while it was even rented to tenants. But since 1924 it has been the property of Mr. and Mrs. A. S. Mitchell who have always maintained it in an immaculate condition. On numerous occasions it has been shown to the public during Old Homes Pilgrimages and Azalea Trail Festivals held from year to year in Mobile. It is indeed gratifying that so many people have had an opportunity to visit this, the most magnificent of Mobile's many ante-bellum mansions.

YESTERHOUSE, Mobile, Alabama

Yesterhouse, nestled amid an eighty-four acre wooded estate in Mobile's exclusive Spring Hill residential district, has the finest double veranda portico of any early mansion in the state. Its eight main columns, as well as those supporting flanking verandas on either side of the dwelling, were adapted from the Tower of the Winds in ancient Greece. The double portico effect is also employed in the courtyard entrance at the rear, only the Doric columns are without decorative capitals. The mansion was built in 1840 by William Dawson, a cotton factor, who came from Charleston, South Carolina. Originally called Palmetto Hall after Dawson's former Charleston home, the mansion has for many decades been one of Mobile's leading social centers. The present owner, Mrs. Eleanor B. Perdue, and the late Dr. W. W. Perdue, purchased the estate thirty-eight years ago from Spring Hill College, which adjoins the grounds. Fifteen house slaves maintained the mansion during Mr. Dawson's lifetime.

Yesterhouse. The narrow spiral staircase in the rear entrance hall (left) is an amazing example of how excellent a secondary stairway can become when good architecture is applied to its design, and quality workmanship to its execution. The rich plasterwork is found in even this rear hall, where the flowingly spiraled medallion becomes a centerpiece of interest.

The main entrance hall (right) is long, tall and very interesting, not only for its delicate plasterwork, but for the entrance door with transom and sidelights of amber, gold and blue glass, each etched with crystal floral decorations. The center glass panels of the double doors are frosted and etched.

170

Yesterhouse. The two free-standing columns and the twenty pilasters in the double parlors are fashioned in the same design as those on the front façade. The plaster cornice trim and the centerpieces are done in extraordinary detail. The plasterwork throughout the mansion, next to that at Gaineswood, is the finest in Alabama. The double marble mantels, imported from Italy, are magnificently carved. The antique furnishings are of select quality, and some pieces, such as the rare Chinese wall rug, are rare collector's items.

171

KIRKBRIDE HOME, Mobile, Alabama

The Kirkbride Home at 104 Theatre Street in Mobile is Alabama's most historic home. It is also one of its most architecturally interesting houses.

The foundation of the old building was part of Fort Conde de la Mobile built in 1717 by the French explorer brothers, Bienville and Iberville who founded the city of Mobile. Thus these foundation stones are part of what is, without a doubt, some of the oldest known masonry in Alabama done by the white man.

The Kirkbride House was not a residence at first. It was a building which served as Mobile's first courthouse and first jail. The heavily barred doors and windows are still part of the rear wing of the house, and masonry three-feet in thickness once covered part of the courtyard around the jail to prevent prisoners from tunneling out.

The house as such is reported to have been built in 1822 by Peter H. Hobart. In 1849 it was purchased by Jonathan Kirkbride who came to Mobile from Mount Holly, New Jersey. Kirkbride made it into an attractive dwelling. It later passed to his son, Edward Kirkbride. Then in 1940 it was bought for a headquarters building by the Historic Mobile Preservation Society and restored in 1944-45 by public donations. During World War II it served as a U. S. Naval officers club.

The contrast of the two level portico is interesting: the ground floor is styled with squatty Tuscan columns, while the second story has fluted Corinthian columns with highly decorative capitals. The crowfoot porch banister adds a delicate touch. The house is built of brick and covered with smooth stucco.

The Kirkbride Home served as Mobile's first courthouse and first jail. Both Tuscan and Corinthian columns are employed in the handsome portico.

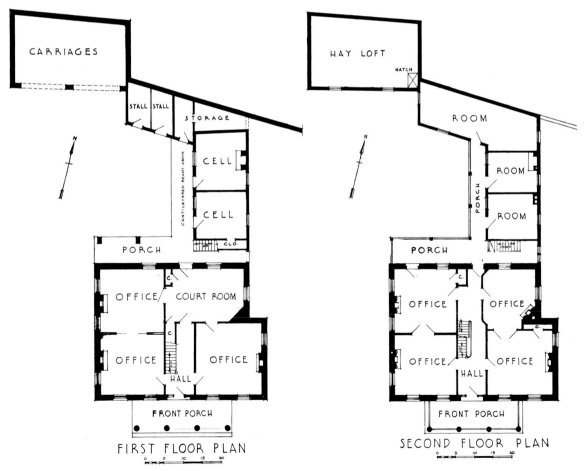

FIRST FLOOR PLAN

SECOND FLOOR PLAN

SEMMES HOUSE, Mobile, Alabama

The Admiral Raphael Semmes House at 802 Government Street is only one of a hundred or more good ante-bellum Mobile homes trimmed with ornamental iron.

This style is known as Creole architecture. It springs from the French influence. When one remembers that Mobile was settled by the French a decade before they moved on to settle New Orleans, it becomes understandable that Alabama's modern seaport metropolis should retain an abundance of the French influence, still popular in the new dwellings of today. However, Mobile does not have the great enclosed courtyards and patios found in many of the New Orleans mansions. This perhaps can be partially explained by the fact that the fires of 1827 and 1938 destroyed entire downtown sections of Mobile where the finer mansions were mostly located.

The Semmes House was built in 1858 by Peter Horta. As was the Creole parti, it was long and narrow, the house having chambers of only one room in width. According to the original plan, the downstairs had a parlor and dining room and a long, narrow hall. Attached to the side rear was the kitchen and the store house. Upstairs were three bedrooms and two servants' rooms. The house was built right up to the sidewalk and has a recessed doorway.

The place was bought by public subscription and donated to Admiral Semmes in 1871 and he lived there until his death in 1878. Shortly after World War II it was purchased by Mr. and Mrs. J. L. Bedsole, Senior, and given as a memorial to the First Baptist Church, next door, in honor of their son, Lieutenant Joseph Linyer Bedsole, Junior, killed in service of his country in 1944. It is now used as a Sunday School department by the church.

By all rights, the state itself should take the necessary steps to make the Semmes Home a state shrine. It could still be used in the manner prescribed by the Bedsoles, and also be honored as a state shrine, along with the homes of General William Crawford Gorgas and Admiral Richmond Pearson Hobson.

Admiral Semmes was a great military man. As commander of the Confederate cruiser *Alabama,* made in Liverpool, England, for the Confederate government, he harassed the Federal shipping lanes for twenty-two months, burning and sinking fifty-seven ships and allowing many others to sail away under ransom bond. It was a great day for the Yankees when, on June 19, 1864, Captain John A. Winslow's *Kearsarge* outfought and sank the *Alabama* in the harbor of Cherbourg, France.

Nowhere in all the annals of Confederate naval history is there a more stirring and exciting chapter than that found in Admiral Semmes' own book, "Service Afloat," written after he retired to his Government Street mansion.

The Admiral Raphael Semmes House, on Mobile's famed Government Street, is a striking example of French influenced Creole architecture.

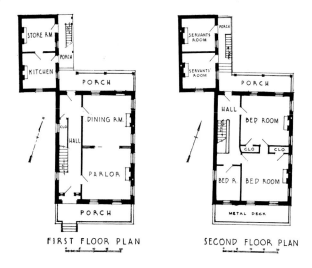

FIRST FLOOR PLAN

SECOND FLOOR PLAN

RICHARDS HOME, Mobile, Alabama

The Richards House is considered to have Mobile's finest display of ornamental ironwork. The small figures illustrated in the porch grillework represent the four seasons. The house was built in 1849 by Charles G. Richards who came to Alabama from Maine and soon amassed a considerable fortune from steamboat operations. The house remained in the Richards family for four generations, and only recently was purchased as a downtown office for a cement firm. It is excellently preserved and there are no indications from the outside that it is used commercially. It is located at 256 North Joachim Street.

CHAPTER VII

Wiregrass Region

Glennville

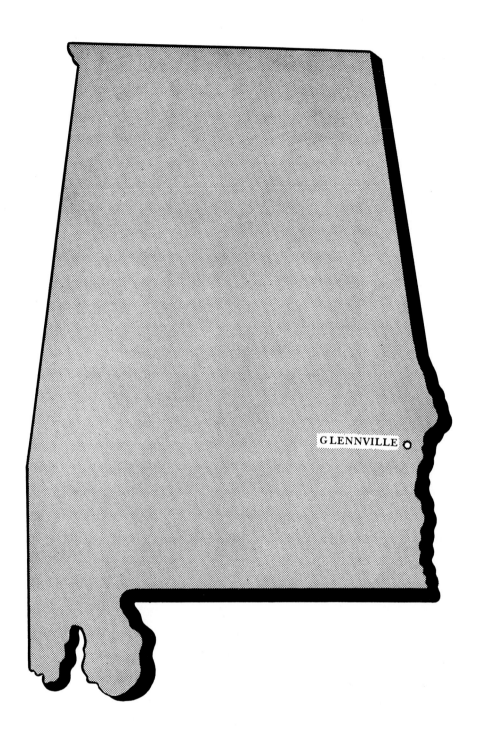

(Wiregrass Region)

GLENNVILLE PLANTATION, Glennville, Alabama

Many a connoisseur of beautiful mansions has chosen Glennville Plantation as the most beautiful in all the state. Certainly, if there is anywhere a pastoral picture of architectural loveliness and refinement it is here at Glennville, located sixteen miles north of Eufaula on the Columbus, Georgia, highway.

The mansion was built during 1842-44, and remains today very much as it was first conceived. The builder was Americus Mitchell who came to the town of Glennville, just to the north of the plantation, in 1841, and settled on land which had been granted to John Mitchell, his grandfather, for Revolutionary War services. It was when he took unto himself a wife, Mary Elizabeth Billingslea of Clinton, Georgia—who came bearing a munificent dowry, that Mitchell bought extensive lands and started the work on the Mitchell home of quality.

Extending from Glennville south to Eufaula was once east Alabama's most thriving plantation region. Great land grants spread out from both sides of the Chattahootchee River, and cotton, grown by the thousands of bales, was floated down to the mouth of the river at Appalachicola, Florida, the largest cotton exporting port in America during these flourishing times.

Glennville Plantation is such a stately house, it is unfortunate that the architect is not known—whether it was Americus Mitchell himself or some peripatetic artisan. However, in the village of Glennville, settled in 1835 by Huguenot Frenchman James E. Glenn, there remain some dozen buildings of the once thriving town and these structures bear similarities to parts of Glennville Plantation—similarities in cornice trim, moulding, entranceways, and column orders. It is said that a house builder named Octanaully had a hand in many of the buildings, but whether or not he helped with Glennville Plantation is not known. Glennville was a very aristocratic place and attracted several hundred daughters and sons of well-to-do planter families to the Glennville Female Academy and the Glennville Collegiate and Military Institute. Faculties of very high caliber were maintained at both institutions, with emphasis upon the classics—language, mathematics, music, rhetoric and the social graces.

Glennville Plantation is one of the nation's finest examples of Greek Revival architecture applied to the mansion type structure. It exactly repeats the Doric order as found in the Parthenon at Athens, Greece, the most perfect Doric structure in all the world. The Doric is the oldest of all the orders, having reached its most definitive perfection during the fifth century, B.C. So, if one would see the glorious beauties of the Parthenon, then look to Glennville Plantation, for here is a mansion exquisitely conceived and masterfully executed. It is truly an architectural gem!

The six magnificently fluted columns taper upward gradually, in accord with Doric design, as they rise to the lofty entablature with its exceedingly beautiful triglyph denticulation. A hipped roof rises at a very low angle from the portico's edge.

The two center columns are more widely spaced than are the others, allowing for a spacious entrance. The entire doorway entrances, both upstairs and down, are recessed into the body of the house. Simple Doric pilasters support broad but plain doorheads. Smaller pilasters frame the sidelights vertically. A balcony with thin, rounded spindles overhangs the veranda, climaxing a most pretentious and awesome view.

The majestic breadth of this same superb planning is also applied inside, for as one enters the commodious central hall, the view commands immediate attention. Dominating the vista is the slowly winding staircase, nothing steep, cumbersome here. The stairs are further enhanced by the curvature of the wainscoting along the wall-side, instead of the more simple and customary baseboard.

The long hall is separated by a wide pilastered arch. The rear of the hall is five feet wider than the front, thus giving a roomlike atmosphere to the surrounding. The double doors leading to the back portico also are sidelighted, but without transom, due to the low sweep of the spiral staircase. The very fine Nineteenth Century early American settee placed beneath the stairwell was once used as a seat for page boys in the senate chamber of the national capitol. It was handed down from Albert Pew Gorham, who sat on the seat as a page, and later served as senator from Maryland, to Mrs. B. B. Comer, Junior, a relative, and present mistress of Glennville Plantation. The original floors are still intact with their wooden pegs.

A rather surprising feature of the house is the additional parlor built octagonal fashion adjoining the end of the rear portico and jutting out as a thing apart from the main body of the house. It offers seclusion and a breezy atmosphere for the long days of hot summer. A kitchen and bedroom are grouped with the parlor and provide a wing for unit living.

In the early 1920's the Franklin Elmores purchased the plantation and mansion which had deteriorated from lack of attention. They set about restoring the original loveliness of not only the mansion and fields, but the fragrant garden as well. And they did wonders for the old place.

Then in 1937 it was bought by Mr. B. B. Comer, Junior, whose father, the Honorable B. B. Comer, Senior, was one of Alabama's greatest governors. The Comers carry on today in the tradition and manner of the earlier days when there were no tangible signs of want, only luxurious surroundings and a vibrant way of life.

The mansion is beautifully landscaped, the veranda receiving the focal attention with the slow-growing, dwarf English boxwood handsomely decorating the foreground, just as it has for over a century now. Glennville Plantation embodies the mythical, almost dreamlike qualities, which romantic novels ascribe to the Old South plantation life. It is almost a dream house, so wondrous are its architectural beauties and charms.

Glennville Plantation. The portico is a replica of the glorified Doric order as found in the Parthenon at Athens, Greece.

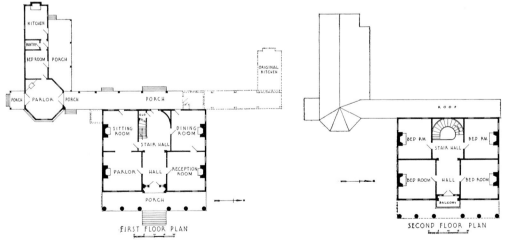

FIRST FLOOR PLAN

SECOND FLOOR PLAN

Glennville Plantation. The slow sweep of the spiral staircase with its paneled wainscoting suggests the elegance of the interior.

CHAPTER VIII

Piedmont Region

Tuskeegee
Auburn

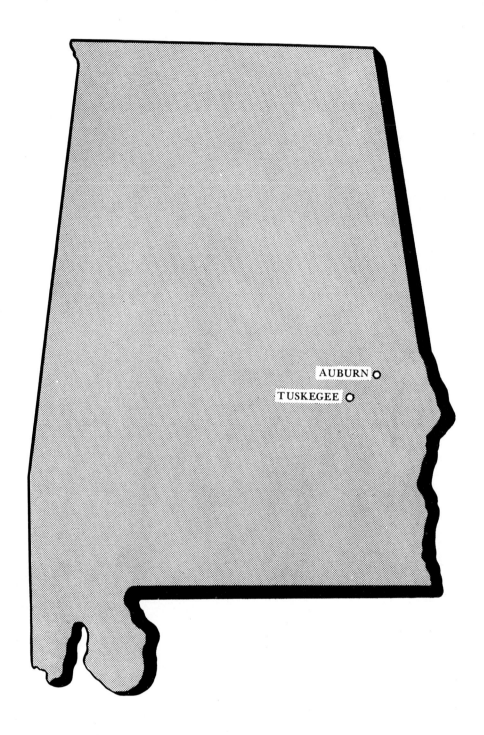

(Piedmont Region)

VARNER-ALEXANDER HOME, Tuskegee, Alabama

The finest mansion of Alabama's Piedmont is the Varner-Alexander Home in Tuskegee, built in 1855-56, by William Varner, a pioneer settler of Macon County. It is reported that Varner himself designed and supervised construction of the mansion, and it is likely that he did since he had been educated in the classics at Harvard University.

It is the state's most elaborate example of the colonnated T-plan, for here the Doric columns are employed on the three sided veranda. The veranda window cornices are very elaborate in Greek decor, while the octagonal cupola bespeaks the South's addition to the popular Greek handbook styles of the period.

The gracious way of life which William Varner fashioned for his family and his descendants is suggested by the elegance of not only double parlors, but also double living rooms. Among the notables entertained here was President Theodore Roosevelt when he came to Tuskegee in 1905, at the invitation of Dr. Booker T. Washington, to visit the world famous Negro school, Tuskegee Institute.

The house has remained in the Varner family and in recent years has been in the possession of the builder's grandson, E. R. Alexander.

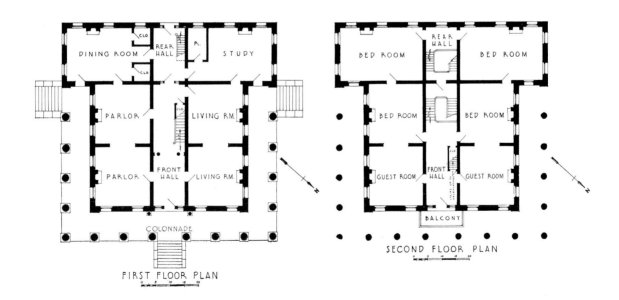

FIRST FLOOR PLAN

SECOND FLOOR PLAN

The Varner-Alexander Home, in magnificent setting, is a noteworthy example of the T-plan mansion. President Theodore Roosevelt once visited here.

FRASIER HOME, Auburn, Alabama

The Frasier House was built in 1854 by Addison Frasier, three miles north of Auburn on Shelton Mill Road. Contractor for the house was Henry Foster who brought with him from his native Kentucky his own carpenters, plasterers and rock masons. Restoration was begun in 1932 by Mr. J. V. Brown and completed after it was purchased in 1941 by Dr. L. N. Duncan, president of Alabama Polytechnic Institute. It is now owned by Dr. and Mrs. Allen M. Pearson, she being the daughter of Dr. and Mrs. Duncan.

Frasier Home. The rear is much like the front, only here it has square pillars. The house, which once was the center of a 2,000 acre plantation, was made of stone and finished with stucco.

188

ADDENDA

Eufaula

SHORTER-UPSHAW HOME,
Eufaula, Alabama

Even though it does not fit within the time element of ante-bellum Alabama, the Shorter-Upshaw Home is included here because of its distinctive example of Greek Revival architecture. Built in 1906, the mansion is Eufaula's residential show-piece.

This close-up shows the fabulous splurging of Corinthian detail in the columns and cornice.

LIST OF SUBSCRIBERS

Mr. & Mrs. Tom Abernethy
Roland L. Adams
Alabama Book Store, Tuscaloosa
Alabama College Library, Montevallo
Alabama Polytechnic Institute
Alabama School of Trades
Alabama State Chamber of Commerce
Mrs. Edward R. Alexander
Mr. & Mrs. Neill Herbert Alford, Jr.
Joseph T. Allen, Jr.
Mr. & Mrs. Miles C. Allgood
Amy's Book Shop
Mrs. Joseph W. Arbuthnot, Sr.
William P. Arrington

Mrs. William T. Badham
Mrs. J. D. Baggett
Allison C. Bailey, Jr.
Mrs. E. H. C. Bailey
Mrs. Sam Rice Baker
Lee Armstead Barclay
Mrs. Lucile Morgan Lancaster Barclay
Mr. & Mrs. Archer P. Bardes
Hudson Barker
Allen L. Bartlett
Mrs. J. E. Beck
Mrs. Samuel Ravaud Benedict
Mary Augusta Bibb
Lee Bidgood
Birmingham Public Library
Rev. Randolph F. Blackford
Algernon Blair
Roy E. Blair
Mrs. George William Bledsoe
Book & Art Shop
The Bookshelf, Birmingham
Miss Margaret Booth
Mrs. Maude Edwards Brittain
Mrs. Richard Brooks
Richard Hail Brown
Mrs. John W. Bryant
Mrs. Merritt Burns, Jr.
Eloise McCain Burton
Mildred Heacock Burton
Hollis Bush

Mrs. Morris Bush
Mrs. O. W. Byrne

Herbert H. Cahoon
Dr. & Mrs. E. V. Caldwell
Miss Kyle Caldwell
Lamar Black Cantelou
Jo Ann Chamberlin
W. N. Chambers
R. B. Chandler
Douglass Clark
Fred W. Clarke
Pressley Welch Cleveland
Mrs. Andrew A. Coffin
G. Arthur Cook
Mrs. Gertrude Russell Coors
Mrs. Doyle W. Cotton
Mr. & Mrs. Thomas Blair Cox
Mr. & Mrs. Asa Cranford
Mr. & Mrs. Charles Rufus Cranford
Elizabeth Bowie Crawford
Walker Reynolds Crook
Mrs. Stephens G. Croom
Mrs. Dexter Cummings
Mrs. Milton K. Cummings

Mrs. John K. Danziger
Amy Livingston Darby
Elton H. Darby
Paul A. Darden
Mrs. Anne Hogue Darrington
Davidson College, Davidson, N.C.
Sally Blake Davidson
William H. Davidson
Mrs. Lillian Davis
Dr. & Mrs. Sumner D. Davis
John G. Dearborn
DeKalb County Library
Mrs. Caldwell Delaney
Detroit Public Library
Edward and Frances De Vesci
Duane Dickson
H. S. Dixon, Jr.
Charles G. Dobbins
Mrs. L. M. Dodds

Rev. Hiram Kennedy Douglass
R. B. Dowdy
Mrs. L. N. Duncan

East Tallahassee Library
Henry M. Edmonds
Mrs. Ida Wallis Elliott
Mrs. Julian Elliott

Roy R. Fair, Jr.
Fairfax Village Library
Mrs. Robert F. Favre
O. H. Finney, Jr.
Robert R. Finney
First White House of the Confederacy
Dr. Gilbert E. Fisher
Mrs. Betty Glover Flye
Mrs. W. B. Folmar
James E. Folsom
Mrs. George L. Foster
Albert R. Frahn
Will F. Franke, Sr. and Jr.
Jean French
Mrs. E. S. Fuller
Johnston Funsten
Reed Funsten

Attorney General Si Garrett
Mrs. Richard Preston Geron
Edward Gene Gibbons
Mrs. Aubrey B. Glass
Colonel & Mrs. Charles Williamson Glover
Mrs. Wm. B. Goodwyn
Mrs. F. J. Gordon
Mrs. Richard Green
Mrs. Hamp Greene
Mrs. Autry Greer
Barton Greer
Mrs. William F. Gresham
Mrs. W. A. Gunter, Jr.

The Hackley Public Library
Mrs. R. B. Hagood
Mrs. J. O. Hain, Jr.
Hale County Library
Mrs. Henry C. Hamilton
Mrs. Louise Sims Hammett
Mrs. A. H. Hammond
Kenneth Hammond
William Bleve Hammond
Mr. & Mrs. John Hancock
Mrs. Hugh Anderson Haralson, **Sr.**
Ben H. Harris
John D. Harris

Seale Harris
Haunted Book Shop
Mr. & Mrs. R. L. Hawkins
Walter Heacock
Mrs. T. B. Hill, Jr.
The Historic Mobile Preservation Society
Robert Hobson
Emma A. Holleman
Mr. & Mrs. M. G. Holleman
Anne and LeRoy Holt
LeRoy Holt
Homewood Library
Mrs. C. Allen Hopkins
George S. Houston Memorial Library
Howard College Library
Mrs. Ernest W. Howell
Dr. & Mrs. T. Brannon Hubbard
Mr. & Mrs. Richard F. Hudson, Jr.
Mr. & Mrs. Frank J. Hughes
Huntsville Public Library
Mayor Grady W. Hurst, Sr.

Margaret B. Ide
Illinois State Library
Ingenieurs-Bureau Ingenegeren-Vrijburg.
    n.v. (Republic of Indonesia)

Doris M. Jacobs
E. Grace Jemison
Robert Jemison, Jr.
Mrs. W. Clyde Jennings
Mrs. Simon M. Jones
Judge Walter B. Jones

Miss Clara Kelley
A. E. Kelly, Jr.
Dr. & Mrs. B. S. Kennedy
Mr. & Mrs. Raleigh B. Kent
Mr. & Mrs. Raleigh B. Kent, Jr.
Dr. Emmett Kilpatrick

Orvice LaBounty
W. E. Lacey
Mrs. Benjamin Washington Lancaster
Earl Miller Lancaster
Mrs. Edwin B. Lancaster
Mrs. Minnie Lucile Morgan Lancaster
Mrs. William Lawrence
Mrs. Matt Lawson
Mary Welch Lee
Mrs. Winston Legge
Mrs. Roy Lightsey
Mrs. John Logan
Long & Gatling

192

S. H. Longshore
Louisville Free Public Library
Loveman's Dept. Store
Mrs. L. T. Lumpkins
Mrs. Mary Lynch
Mr. & Mrs. R. H. Lynch

Mrs. Forrest McConnell
Mr. & Mrs. LeRoy McEntire
Mrs. Neal S. McGaffey
Mrs. William H. McGowen
Mrs. Mildred Russell McKeithen
Mrs. Lauch Bethea McLaurin
Paul M. McLendon, Jr.
Dr. & Mrs. John D. McLeod
Hope Miller McMillan
Mrs. Hobart Amory McWhorter

B. Dale Malan
Mrs. Fred H. Marshall, Jr.
Mrs. Evelyn Tyson Martin
Dr. & Mrs. John A. Martin
John J. Mason
Barnett H. Matthews
Mr. & Mrs. Welborn Matthews
James A. Megginson
Methodist Publishing House
John M. Miller, IIIrd.
Mrs. A. S. Mitchell
Mr. & Mrs. Sam S. Mitchell
Sidney A. Mitchell
The Mobile Press Register
Miss M. Elizabeth Moffat
Montgomery Chamber of Commerce
Montgomery County Library
Mr. & Mrs. Ryall Morgan
Mr. & Mrs. J. L. Morrison

Neeley's—Books
Naomi and Howard Nelson
Dr. & Mrs. Robert Nelson, Jr.
Glenn Nichols
Katie Files Nick
Leon Nolen

Frances Cleveland Oliver
Mrs. Samuel Clark Oliver
Mrs. A. O. Olson
Mr. & Mrs. Woodfin Owens

Albert L. Patterson
Joseph B. Pearce
Pearson, Tittle and Narrows
Mr. & Mrs. Harold Piatt

Lieutenant General & Mrs. Lewis Andrew
  Pick
W. E. Pickens, Jr.
Mrs. W. M. Pierce
Mrs. Cameron Plummer
Mrs. Amy D. Pottery
Mrs. Lindsay James Powell
Preferred Life Assurance Society
Mr. & Mrs. Julius L. Poritz
Mrs. A. J. Price
Judge Annie Lola Price
Mrs. W. T. Price
Mrs. John Blevins Privett

Mr. & Mrs. G. W. Ragsdale
Ed E. Reid
Mrs. Winbourn Remson
Mrs. Georgina K. Reynolds
Miss Hannah E. Reynolds
Mr. & Mrs. Walker Reynolds
Lucy L. Riddle
Mrs. Erma Cramer Robinson
Mrs. Frances Simms Rockwell
Frances McKenzie Rogers
William Alfred Rose
Rosemount Antiques
Mr. & Mrs. W. M. Rozelle, Jr.
Mr. & Mrs. W. M. Rozelle, Sr.
Mrs. B. B. Rudolph, Sr.
Mr. & Mrs. Joseph B. Rush
Edward P. Russell
Dr. Archibald Rutledge

Mildred Reynolds Saffold
Paul Sanderson—Books
Curt Schmidt
Mary Wingfield Scott
Dr. David F. Sellers
Mrs. S. T. Shank
Alice and Lee Sharp
Mrs. Martha Lyman Shillito
Mrs. Clyde L. Sibley
Raymond Sizemore
Smith & Hardwick, Inc.
Mr. & Mrs. Esles Smith, Sr.
Harriet Lyon Smith
Mrs. Mallory Reynolds Smith
Mrs. Mattie Gilbert Smith
Captain & Mrs. Randolph Smith, USMCR
Mrs. W. Lindsay Smith
Mr. & Mrs. Walter Lindsay Smith, Jr.
Mrs. Thomas L. Speck
In Memoriam Annie Greene Stackhouse
State of Alabama, Archives & History Dept.

Harrison R. Steeves, Jr.
Katharine Elsberry Steiner
Mrs. Helen Koethen Stewart
Mrs. Clifford F. Stiles
Mrs. B. A. Stockton
Miss Nannette Stockton
Mrs. W. O. Stoddard
Stokes & Stockwell Book Shop
Clyde H. Strickland
Studio Book Shop
James Sulzby
Frances Rudulph Summers
Mrs. Joseph Jordan Swenson

Talladega High School
Talladega Public Library
Talladega Study Club
Mrs. Ruby Pickens Tartt
Darcey T. Tatum, Jr.
Evan M. Terry
Dr. Charles Alston Thigpen
Mr. & Mrs. J. Innes Thornton
Dr. & Mrs. William Getz Thuss
C. Swift Treadwell
Tim L. Treadwell, Jr.
George P. Turner
Tuscaloosa County Library
Frances Patteson Tutwiler
Mrs. Archie Tyson
John Caius Tyson
Mrs. Jones A. Tyson

University of Alabama Library
University of Kansas

Miss Anne Kendrick Walker
T. O. (Tillie) Walker
George Wallace

Hon. George Platt Waller
W. T. Warren
Mrs. Carroll B. Waterman
Mrs. John B. Waterman
Mr. & Mrs. Joseph A. Waters
Mrs. James F. Watts
Mrs. Virginia Norwood Watts
Mrs. Robert Stone Weatherly
Rosalie Weaver
Ariel Welch
Barbara Anne Welch
Ethel Roberta Welch
Gorton T. Welch
Mr. & Mrs. Nat Welch
Oliver William Welch
Mr. & Mrs. W. P. Welch
Willie W. Welch
Welch's Book Shop
Boyd H. Wells
John A. Wetzel
E. Weyhe
Clark Whistler
Mr. & Mrs. Norman L. White
White House Association
Mr. & Mrs. James Vivian Whitfield
Miss Maria Whitson
J. Streeter Wiatt
Willard Library, Evansville, Indiana
Mrs. Mary Rogers Williams
Wallace E. Williams
Mrs. Charles A. Wolfes
Mrs. Amelia Russell Wood
May Crommelin Wood
T. A. Wootton

Dr. & Mrs. John Xan

Fletcher L. Yarbrough

194

INDEX OF MANSIONS